A
HISTORY
&
BIBLIOGRAPHY
OF THE
ROYCROFT PRINTING
SHOP

SECOND EDITION

BY
PAUL MCKENNA

TONA GRAPHICS
GRAND ISLAND, NEW YORK

To Alexander Nesbitt
Friend and Teacher

Library of Congress number: 81-86148
ISBN 0-939892-00-6

All correspondence should be directed to:
TONA GRAPHICS
P.O. Box 58
Grand Island, NY 14072
Tele & fax: (716)773 4059

PREFACE TO THE SECOND EDITION

Ten years have passed since the publication of the first edition of this work. The Arts and Crafts Movement has continued to attract new collectors, some more history has been recorded and the Roycroft artifacts have been getting the attention they have long deserved.

This second edition is a response to the inquiries that started during the last year. I hadn't intended to do this second edition but there was no other book on the printing shop available to collectors. The first editions were commanding premium prices on the out-of-print market when they could be located and few copies were being found at prices under seventy-five dollars.

The additions and corrections noted in this edition of the bibliography were forwarded by interested dealers and collectors. I especially thank Jay T. Johnson of Dallas for his major contributions. I really thought we would find many more limited editions but they remain mysteries-much to my surprise. When I finished the first edition it was offered as the beginning of a continuing search for the missing editions and a text to record corrections to the bibliography. No pertinent new information of the major Roycroft personnel has been uncovered. I still treat the material produced after 1915 as relatively minor again in this edition but can now offer some information on the subject matter of the post 1915 books. Many are on occult or non-conformist religions. Jon Weekly of Mahoney and Weekly Booksellers shed light on these Roycroft printings. He remembered that his late partner Tom Mahoney had purchased the Larkin library and that many of the titles were also occult and non-conformist. The Larkins were always associated with the Hubbard family and we can conjecture that Bert Hubbard was able to obtain printing orders from friends of the Larkins who wrote in these subject areas. This supposition makes sense.

PREFACE TO THE FIRST EDITION

I regard the Roycroft Shop and its product as a distinct phase of Americana—in much the same manner I regard Currier and Ives, the Rogers Group or mission furniture—something that had its day, left its influence and passed . There is no need to praise or condemn these steps in the evolution of Americana, or to try to explain them.

Dard Hunter [1]

Dard Hunter was right. The Roycroft Shop had its day, but its day, unlike that of Currier and Ives, has not been documented. What the Roycroft Printing Shop accomplished was important in the history of American book making and graphic design. However, its efforts have been ignored or belittled until recently so I hope that this work will generate a greater interest in, and an appreciation of, its place in our graphic arts history.

Much of the history of Elbert Hubbard and the Roycroft enterprise inaccurately depicts his involvement in book making. How much did he know about books and how much did he care to know? What was his goal? Did he plan to establish a training ground and meeting place for the creative in the arts and crafts or did he just want to insure an outlet for his own writings?

I'll try to answer these questions in this study. I am convinced that the shop was much more than May Morris' description of it as ". ....
that obnoxious imitator of my father."[2]

The problems encountered in compiling this history and bibliography were considerable. There exists one ledger, that for the accounting year 1909/10, and few other records that could be substantiated. The files and records of the shop were sold as scrap paper at the beginning of the Second World War. Much of the material published about the shop has been innocently based on material written by Elbert Hubbard and much of the research time on this project has been consumed in refuting and correcting erroneous information. The only sources that I recommend are Champney's *Art and Glory*,[3] Hamilton's *As Bees In Honey Drown*[4] and Dirlam/Simmons *Sinners, This is East Aurora*.[5] These sources do have accurate information on Elbert Hubbard and do cover the press and its publications to some extent.

The bibliography posed unique problems. The catalogs issued by the press were often at odds with the books they advertised. Variant editions abound and the limitation statements in the books are usually not in agreement with the information in the catalogs. Binding styles do not correspond with those advertised for each edition in design and/or availability. Volumes advertised in one catalog as being almost sold out ("A few volumes left" was the favored expression) were still offered in successive catalogs without the previous warning of impending unavailability. Were these extra books found in the basement or a new edition? Was "A few volumes left" sales hype? It meant searching for as many copies of the suspicious titles as could be found and collating each.

The limitation statements are also suspect and this has been covered in a chapter "Are They Real?".

The Bibliography is divided into two parts. The Roycroft Printing Shop existed from 1895 to 1941 but it ceased to produce much interesting work after 1915. This year has been chosen as the cut-off point for the major entry listings for that reason and because 1915 was the year of the deaths of Elbert and Alice Hubbard—the stimulus for what good work the press had been doing.

I have not used the standard bibliographical methods for those books produced between 1896-1915. I have resorted to a simpler and more descriptive method. Entries are listed alphabetically by titles rather than authors within year of publication since after the first two years no accurate precedence of publication could be made.

Pages are given in actual folio number printed; that is, if the page number of an entry is given as 115, the last printed page number in that entry is 115.

I have not noted blanks, half-titles, etc. unless they are important to the correct identification of an edition.

Dimensions are given in inches since many collectors using this material will not be familiar with the metric system. The dimensions given are for page size and not binding. The handmade and uncut papers used in the books will show a variance and allowance must be given in measuring. There are sufficient differences between editions to allow elimination of small dimension changes as points of comparison.

Unless a particular binding is a unique point of identification for a separate edition, bindings have not been noted as separate offerings.

Type faces used in the books are very important. The faces employed are the best guide for identifying the editions in multiple editions. Every effort has been made to correctly identify the types used. Most are given their foundry or Monotype names since American Type Founders, Keystone Type Foundry and The Monotype Corporation were the suppliers to the shop.

The titles issued after 1915 are given as short title listings. Very few interesting books were done after that year and those few that are interesting have been given a fuller treatment. After 1915 the shop was almost exclusively committed to vanity and straight commercial printing and the unique Roycroft "style" is rarely seen.

There are many titles done by the shop after 1915 that have not been located. Again, there are no records of the vanity printings and all copies of these press runs were probably turned over to the client. Only copies that were inscribed and given as gifts to the Hubbards or a Roycroft employee and ended up in the Roycroft museum have been seen.

Those entries defining limited editions as "a few", borrowing the wording of the Roycrofters, means that we can be sure that a limited edition was produced but an example has not yet been located for inspection. " A few" usually means one hundred to one hundred ten copies if all those other limited editions examined are any clue.

More of the limited editions and new post-1915 titles are still being found and it is hoped that this work will bring more attention to the search.

A short title list is given of serials, catalogs and pamphlets issued by the press. Bibliographical description of each of these is unnecessary except that variant cover designs are noted. Please note that a pamphlet has been placed in the main bibliographical section if it can be considered as having literary merit and is not just an advertising piece. Also, not all of the catalogs issued by the press have been noted. Several issues of the same catalog were offered with variant covers or with just an added editorial or picture section which was not unique to that issue. Those catalogs noted constitute those which are important in the history of the press and offer original information.

Finally, anyone who attempts a serious study in any subject area is

viii

lost without those who contribute their time and knowledge. I have
many to thank. Mr. and Mrs. Charles Hamilton kindly shared their
knowledge of the Hubbard family with me and arranged introductions
to those who could add to this study. The late Mrs. Virginia Vidler, historian of the Town of Aurora, provided much needed assistance helping me scan the material in the town's collection and encouraging me to
keep digging for facts as she had in her career as a successful writer.

Professor Douglas G. Greene kindly gave me access to his notes on W.
W. Denslow's association with the Roycroft shop and Elbert Hubbard.

Robert Volz, Curator of the Chapin Collection, Williams College, provided access to the marvelous collection of Roycroft material he had
assembled while associated with the University of Rochester.

William Loos, Rare Book Librarian of the Buffalo and Erie County
Library, was always quick to inform me of any Roycroft material he had
uncovered in his organization of that library's Roycroft holdings.

Roycroft collectors such as Richard Blacher, Boyce Liddell, Jean-
Francois Vilain and Dale Weber were a great help in reporting new editions or variants they have discovered. They have been a great and sympathetic aid to me in this study.

Finally, I am fortunate in having a wife, Janet McKenna, who is not
only an excellent reference librarian but was an editor and has given me
the benefit of both of her areas of expertise. I also thank her for her
patience.

THE PEOPLE

Any history of the Roycroft Printing Shop or Roycroft Press as it is now commonly known must deal with Elbert Hubbard. Hubbard has been well covered in Champney and Hamilton so we will give only that biographical data pertinent to understanding his approach to literature, publishing and people.

Hubbard's relationship to others is the most important aspect in understanding him and the Roycroft Press. To me, Hubbard's personal history in his mature years is one of reaction to others.

Elbert Hubbard was born on June 19, 1856 in Bloomington, Illinois to Dr. Silas and Juliana Frances Hubbard. Dr. Hubbard had left a reasonably successful practice in Buffalo, New York in that year for an uncertain future in Illinois. Elbert Greene Hubbard was their third child. Their first child, Charles, had twisted his spine in a fall and was crippled. Their second child, Hannah Frances, had been born in 1853.

After Elbert's birth, the family moved to the village of Hudson and eventually settled across from the new Baptist church. The doctor's practice picked up among local farmers and he was satisfied with the situation although payment was often in produce rather than cash. Juliana Hubbard may have had different feelings about life in rural Illinois. Two years after Elbert's birth she lost premature twin boys and when Elbert was three and a half, Charlie died. Charlie was his mother's favorite and his death changed her from a quiet even-tempered woman to one of emotional instability.

She gave birth to a daughter named Anna Miranda but always called "Daisy"-the name given her by young Elbert. A third daughter born in 1864 was named Mary and her last child, a daughter named Honor, was born in 1868.

Elbert's boyhood was ordinary enough. He paid as little attention to school work as possible but he couldn't avoid religion which he got in triple doses from his father's family prayers, the nearby Baptist church and from the Bible readings that formed a part of the school curriculum of the day. He never submitted to baptism and in his later writings took the position that religion was a crutch which lessened a man's self-reliance.

Although he could keep his distance from religion he couldn't stay away from horses. The first twelve dollars he earned from his chores and errands went for the purchase of a horse. In the later Roycroft years he always said that he preferred the company of a good horse to that of many a man he'd met and often spoke of his early ability with horses.

He left school in his sixteenth year after deciding to be a farmer. His father's profession didn't interest him and he was not pushed in that direction by his parents. He loved animals, hard work and outdoor living and he was handy enough to be welcome on the local farms as a hired hand. He would have happily settled for the life of a farmer on his own land but a visit from a relative changed his life.

Justin Weller, Silas Hubbard's nephew and partner of his wife's brother John Larkin was impressed with young Elbert and offered him a job. Larkin and Weller made soap and they were looking for someone to cover a route in that part of rural Illinois with their unique selling plan.

Soap was just becoming a product for mass production and distribution in the Midwest and farm families were now ready to purchase soap rather than make their own. Weller invited Elbert to sell soap door to door so Elbert painted up the family wagon in bright colors, added the company name and hit the road.

Within three years he had retired the family wagon and was using trains and hired teams. Although the selling plan employed by Larkin and Weller was popular it still had to be sold and "Bert" Hubbard sold more than anyone else in the company. He liked meeting people, had a sense of humor and was a good storyteller. As a commercial traveler he affected the loud dress of the drummer but found more company in a book than a saloon. His reminiscences of this part of his life are accurate and his reading at this point in his life shows that he was part of that movement in the midwest towards radicalism.[6] He read Darwin, Emerson and Ingersoll and would later reprint the basic work of Emerson and Ingersoll.

In 1875 Hubbard had to make a decision. The Larkin-Weller partnership was breaking up and both parties sought his services. When the partnership was dissolved it had been decided that Weller would keep the Chicago factory and the midwest territory. Larkin would build a plant in Buffalo, New York and have all of the territory east of Detroit.

Hubbard chose to join John Larkin and at the age of nineteen he moved to Buffalo and continued selling in his new territory with success. In 1881 he married Bertha Crawford whom he had met in the mid-west. They set up house in Buffalo and Bertha gave birth to their first son-Elbert II, later also known as Bert.

Three years after the marriage Hubbard was attracted to the local horse breeding center, East Aurora, New York, where he bought a house and a small parcel of land. After a day at the Larkin Works he would make the twenty mile trip home by train and relax at the local exercise tracks. He started to exercise horses and was soon buying and selling trotters.

The turning point came in 1890. He started writing, and despite his later claim to having been the book, music, art and drama critic of The Chicago Times, this obviously was his first attempt at self-expression. It was called *The Man: A Story of Today* and was written under the pen name of Asphasia Hobbs. Published by J. S. Ogilvie as part of their Sunnydale Series, it was awful but it did contain hints of the changes in Elbert Hubbard.

The basic story was of Asphasia Hobbs, spinster, and her relationship to The Man, a veritable fount of knowledge. The Man, obviously Hubbard, comments on everything including the basic goodness of women-but not wives. This woman/wife relationship could signal the partition in Hubbard's mind between his wife Bertha and Alice Moore.

Another clue to Hubbard's evolution was a letter prefacing The Man. Addressed to "John Bilkerson of Hustler & Co." it indicated his changed feelings about business.

He arranged to sell his interest in Larkin and announced his intention of enrolling in Harvard. His academic career was brief. He entered Harvard as a special student in the Fall of 1893 and withdrew before the end of the semester. He re-enrolled the following semester but again stayed less than a semester. The only things he got out of his stay at Harvard, according to Hubbard, were a prejudice against dullness and unimaginativeness and the idea for the Little Journeys. A trip to Concord while at Harvard, so he said, gave him the idea to write about the literary greats. In 1894 he sailed for England to begin his tour of the homes of the literary greats. Upon his return to East Aurora he compiled his first Little Journey and started another novel, No Enemy (But Himself). The year 1894 is significant for more than the beginning of the Little Journey series that would bring Hubbard to public notice. In that year he fathered two daughters, Katherine and Miriam. Katherine was born to his wife Bertha and Miriam to Alice Moore.

Alice Moore was teaching school in East Aurora when Elbert Hubbard met her in 1889. Hubbard described her in a Philistine article in 1901 and would have the reader believe that he met her while lecturing in Philadelphia.

Chapney feels that Alice Moore was a friend of Bertha Hubbard before she met Elbert. This seems likely and there is little doubt that he was infatuated with this intelligent, self-sufficient woman. The best account of their relationship is in Hamilton's *As Bees in Honey Drown*.

Alice left the child with her sister and brother-in-law, the William Woodwards of Buffalo, and took a teaching job in Denver, Colorado.

Hubbard had agreed to pay five dollars a week for Miriam's support but in 1901 Woodward filed suit charging that he had spent three thousand dollars to support the child and had not received the promised child support from Elbert Hubbard.[7]

Alice returned to Buffalo, picked up Miriam and headed for Concord, Massachusetts. Elbert and Bertha were divorced on January 11,1904. Hubbard was lecturing in Washington when his son Bert informed him by telegraph that the final divorce decree had been issued. He went on to Philadelphia, sent for Alice and they were married on January 18, 1904.

Bertha Hubbard disappeared from the Roycroft scene and Alice Moore Hubbard returned to East Aurora to face the community and to take her place in the Roycroft community. She quickly proved herself an astute businesswoman and took over the operation of the printing shop as general manager. Alice and Elbert were a balanced pair. Where Elbert was impetuous, Alice was reserved; where he was too generous she was too frugal. He took the part of the father-patron while she watched the books.

They died together on the Lusitania. Hubbard had talked about their possible deaths because of German warnings that the ship was considered a legitimate war target. Hubbard had said in his last letter to his employees that "We shall be away two months or longer, perhaps."[8]

It was said in Roycroft circles that the Kaiser had ordered the ship sunk to avoid having to face Elbert Hubbard and explain why he, the Kaiser, wanted war. It was also said that the sinking was in revenge for Hubbard's pamphlet, *Who Opened the Gates of Hell? The Kaiser Did!* We now know the true story of the sinking of the ship but these stories had credence at the time. If the Kaiser had met Hubbard it would have done Hubbard more good than the Kaiser. By 1915 Hubbard was fast fading in popular appeal. He had turned to the large commercial/industrial interests for his support and wrote in their defense against those demanding a public accounting from the trusts, etc.

The unquestioned obedience expounded in *The Message to Garcia* was no longer popular with the younger part of the population and his audience was fast aging with him.

Hubbard probably would have tried to phase out the Roycroft Printing Shop along with the other shops in the enterprise. It was much too big and could not support itself unless drastic cuts were made in personnel and equipment. I can only conjecture that Hubbard would have continued to write for his own audience and accept commissions to represent the interests of those who were his clients at the end of his life.

He was remembered by his friends and enemies for what he had been. He had been an honest, intelligent, generous man who had a talent for writing popular essays with some wit. He also hurt people by not understanding that wit can hurt people if used without thought.

His relationship with his friends and enemies shows how he succeeded and failed as the Roycroft enterprise grew.

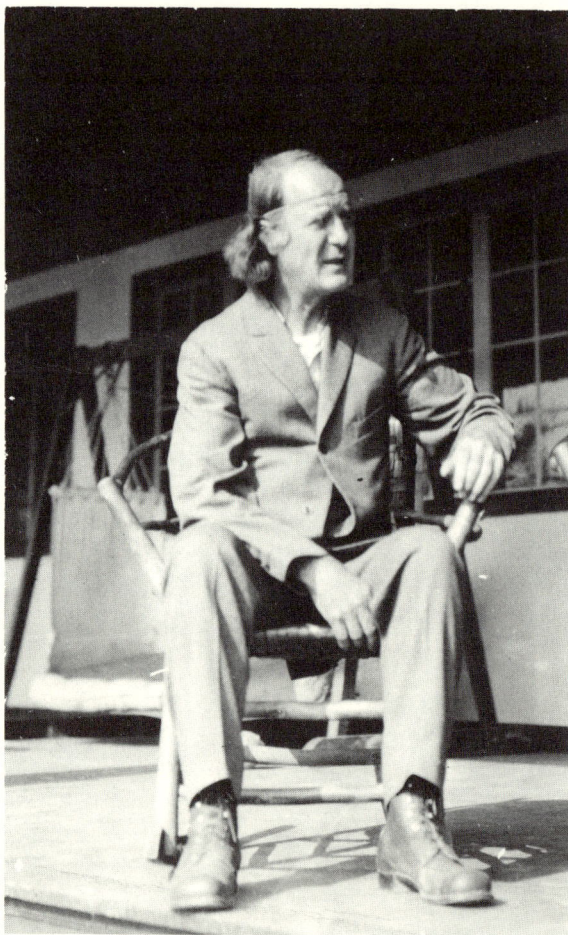

The "Fra" in 1915: the year of his death

FRIENDS AND ENEMIES

Anyone in the public eye has friends and enemies beyond the normal measure. Elbert Hubbard was no exception and his behavior on occasion left him vulnerable to his enemies. He was vilified and ridiculed in the national and local press by his enemies while he was praised and defended with equal vigor by his friends.

There was something in Hubbard's personality that invited favorable response as evidenced by his success as a soap salesman. But as a literary figure and publisher his ego dominated his natural friendliness and fairness and led to considerable bitterness among those who broke with him. His success because of and later without them may have fueled the anger but too often Elbert Hubbard was the cause of the breakup.

We will note some of those who were involved in literary and/or personal relationships with him. They were friends and enemies and we'll start with the enemies because they came first.

Harry P. Taber was the first to involve himself professionally with Hubbard and lose. Taber was the true founder of the Roycroft Printing Shop and exemplifies the innovator who has historically been bought out and then thrown out. We'll detail the business relationship between Taber and Hubbard later. Harry P. Taber remained Hubbard's enemy and debunker long after Hubbard's death. We know that all that Taber charged to Hubbard is not true but he was the first victim of Hubbard's ego.

Another early victim of Elbert Hubbard's ego was Walter Blackburn Harte, an acquaintance from Hubbard's Boston days and the proprietor of The Fly Leaf, another small magazine.

The controversy about the relationship between Hubbard and Harte has never been clearly resolved. Did Hubbard invite Harte to East Aurora as a full partner and editor of The Philistine or did he trap Harte into dissolving his popular little magazine and thus eliminate some competition? Did Harte impose himself on Hubbard and have to be given one of Hubbard's famous "one way tickets on the four o'clock train?"

Harte was quoted in the first issue of The Philistine and his work

8

appeared or he was mentioned in two other issues in 1895. The April 1896 issue of The Phil announced that Mr. Harte would join the magazine. The exact wording is:

ANNOUNCEMENT . . . The Society of the Philistines has made an arrangement with Mr. Walter Blackburn Harte, the Editor and Publisher of The Fly Leaf, Boston, Massachusetts to acquire and incorporate The Fly Leaf with The Philistine.

Under this arrangement the services of Mr. Harte will be retained by the Society and he will henceforth devote his time and efforts to furthering the interests of The Philistine and the Roycroft Printing Shop.

After April 1st Mr. Harte's address will be East Aurora, N.Y. All unexpired subscriptions to The Fly Leaf will be filled by THE PHILISTINE East Aurora, N.Y.

"Walter Blackburn Harte has engaged board at the Widow Blannerhassett's, second door east of the blacksmith shop. At Johnson's grocery last night Harte beat old Si Emery three straight games at checkers-and that is no small matter."[9]

There have been claims that the actual contract or agreement between Harte and Hubbard exists and has been seen. I have not seen that document but I have seen this letter which is worth quoting in full.[10]

The Fly Leaf is Distinctive among all the Bibelots
Floodlights, Philadelphia

THE FLY LEAF
269 St. Botolph Street,
Boston, Mass. 10th March. (P.M.) 1896

Conducted by Walter Blackburn Harte.

My Dear Hubbard,

I am writing this in haste to get into the mail before midnight so that it will reach you by tomorrow evening's delivery.

I have been out all day long on business and did not receive yours cf the 9th inst. with the proposition until this evening when I got home late and found it awaiting me. I have thought it carefully over, & sent you an acknowledgment by telegraph as follows: "will accept on certain conditions of permanence. Explanatory letter follows".

This is as clear as I could make it in a telegram. I will now explain the considerations I have in mind in a few clear and simple paragraphs so that you can appreciate my situation at a glance.

The first consideration is the permanence of the arrangement. Any arrangement which did not promise some permanence for me allowing for the possibility of severe reverses or decision to quit business altogether, would scarcely justify the move, especially if it included any publicity.

You offer an arrangement to last until July first. I could not get away from here until April first, as I am obliged to pay rent until then. Then I have got to sell my furniture at a sacrifice to get away, & that takes a little time. To pack also takes a little time, and I am now under way with The Fly Leaf for April-half the matter is in type, & certain advertising arrangements have to be carried out, or I shall be liable. So that if I joined you on April first, or a little earlier, this would make the arrangement pending only for three months. Then you say "If on July1st you want to go back to Boston I'll pay your R.R. fare back." If I do not think I should want to, and could, stay on in East Aurora, I should not want to make the move, because it would not be judicious.

There are two sides to this. One is this. If on July 1st. you should decide not to continue the arrangement, on our arrangement of division of profits, I should be in a bad position, as July is a bad time of year, and moreover I should have been to expense without gaining any advantage. As you put it the arrangement may come to an end on July first, if you wish to terminate it for any reason. You know me & something of my ability and experience in this business, both as a writer and as an advertisement writer, a general office man. I know you and if I did not think I should like you I should not dream of trying to work with you, because unless men can get on together & understand each other there can be no prospect for one or the other in such a relation.

I thought you had given this important matter due consideration before making any suggestion to me, as all business arrangements must necessarily subsist upon this feeling of liking & understanding that carries permanence with it. I should not wish to enter into an arrangement to go to work until July first, and then confront the possibility of another change that would certainly be to my disadvantage. In entering upon a new employment I should not want to feel that it's a temporary arrangement liable to cease in three months. This clause in your letter makes the proposition indefinite & impermanent. I am anxious for permanence in my work, and if I incorporated The Fly Leaf in The Philistine I should look for a permanent relation, to be interrupted only by failure, or the stopping of publication.

It would be a distinct detriment to me to incorporate The Fly Leaf in The Philistine on a probationary basis, which might end on July first, especially if I were identified with the change, as proposed. If after three months my connection ceased I should appear in a bad light and be in a worse position to obtain employment than now. It would look as if I had failed to make The Fly Leaf go, and had then shown inability to do what was required on The Philistine. It would be injurious to have any sort of announcement of a combination of the two magazines if this were followed in three months by the news of my sudden retirement from the combination-concern. If The Fly Leaf alone failed to support itself it would be all right and dignified enough to let it drop. There could be no gossip about that and I should go out with a fair record. The failure would not in any way reflect upon me since it would only be due to lack of capital.

But if I joined you for three months, and the fact of my connection was announced, then I withdraw, it would appear to all in the business that I was incapable of doing the work required. I understood from your first letter that your arrangement with Taber was to pay him just enough for his living, and to divide profits.

Then I understood in your proposition of a consolidation we were to work together & get out of it what there was in it-on the division of returns, & division of cost. I did not & do not know whether this would insure the means of a living, even with strict economy. But the arrangement, I understood, was to be permanent. Unless of course the business lost money right along, when it would not pay to continue and I should be content to share in the fortunes of the concern. If the returns from the magazine did not justify the salary you propose to pay me I should not like to take it, as I should not feel I was earning it. Then if the returns did not give either of us a livelihood at all I could not expect you to need me or continue. But this arrangement of sharing would be more desirable than drawing a salary which was not earned by the enterprise. I should not be at all comfortable under any arrangement by which you paid me a salary which the business could not justify. And such an arrangement in the nature of things would not be permanent.

If your returns are good enough to justify $15 a week, which is quite an expense for one of these monthlies, then on a partnership arrangement I could hope to make my living and should prefer to work for the success of the enterprise, & take more or less as our efforts met with success or reverses. This was what I understood you to propose in your first letter.

But the letter just to hand makes the offer a temporary engagement for three months employment, which appears to me something of a risk. The inducement of any such arrangement to me is the chance of working to help build up a paying thing, in which I should be repaid for my efforts by my share of the returns. In a word, if I could make a living & work for more on the basis of a permanent partnership the offer has strong attractions, but to effect a combination for three months' employment, with uncertainty of tenure at the end of it, seems to me too great a risk on my side. Just three months work at the Philistine then a sudden break would create a prejudice against me in many newspaper quarters, & I should not gain by it, financially. It would not help me in getting fresh employment.

The Fly Leaf is making progress & I think it only needs a little capital to establish itself. The longer it runs the more easy it will be to interest people & the News Co. may do better by it if they see it swimming. New subscribers are coming in at the rate of one or two a day, and this may improve with time and working up. We have now about 150 subscribers we have had no means of getting them, but correspondence & samples. I've only lately begun to work up this end by circularizing, & with assurance of continuity I think people would come in better. They are scared of new things.

The News Co. handles from 2500 to 2800 copies, & as the thing gets better known more Dealers will handle it in different cities, & give it a show. At first many cities were not covered, but I am in communication with dealers in different places and stir them and interest them.

Harte came to East Aurora in December 1896 and stayed fourteen days, departing on January 1,1897. Hubbard remembered Harte in his Manifesto -"Next Walter Blackburn Harte came down upon me, & he was the finest o' the lot. He remained in East Aurora two weeks (lacking one day) & didn't do a thing while he was here but tie fire-crackers to my coat-tail. He then towlsed his hair like a boofay artist, curst in falsetto, & rushed into "footlights" and another sheet like it, called "The Critic", telling why East Aurora was no place for a man of genius, and declaring I was a big What-D'ye-Call-lt."

Hubbard took pot-shots at Harte long after the man was dead. Hubbard's reaction leads me to believe that Harte was the wronged party. He was not the first, of course, and he certainly was not the last.

Hubbard soon acquired two more enemies of far more prominence than Walter Blackburn Harte and with more power to hit back.

Hubbard published work by George Bernard Shaw and Rudyard Kipling and bastardized each man's work. He gained an unrelenting enemy in Shaw and was sued by Kipling.

The copyright situation at the turn of the century encouraged pirating of non-American authors by American publishers. Thomas Bird Mosher never paid royalties nor did most of the commercial publishers unless they saw advantages over their competition in gaining the favor of a foreign author.

The only recourse available to a foreign author was to arrange for the publication in the United States of a limited edition of a work and thus secure copyright protection in this country. Kipling protected most of his work this way but that did not stop Elbert Hubbard.

Hubbard not only published a copyrighted work without permission but he changed it! He first published Kipling's *Last Chanty* as *The Dipsy Chanty* in The Philistine of December 1895. Why he changed the title is anybody's guess, but his introduction to the work is flattering to Kipling. We may suppose that the appearance of the work in book form prompted Kipling to initiate a suit through his American publishers. Kipling asked for surrender of all unsold copies, payment of $47.50 plus costs of the suit. Hubbard agreed to settle by withdrawing the book from sale and paying the legal fees. Kipling got $75.00 for his attorneys and 169 copies of the pirated work. Hubbard got the last laugh.

He wrote a letter to the New York Times Saturday Review[12] in answer to an article about the suit. He boasted that he had agreed to withdraw the book because he had sold all that he could and he agreed to pay Kipling's legal fees because it did not matter whether he had to pay his or the other fellow's lawyer. He was right about selling enough. Kipling obviously did not know that Hubbard had printed three editions of around 950 copies (see bibliography) and that 169 were the remaining copies of the three editions.

Hubbard probably made more money on George Bernard Shaw but he gained an unforgiving enemy.

He wrote to Shaw inquiring about copyright and/or permission to publish On Going To Church which had appeared in the Savoy Magazine of January 1896. Shaw replied that as far as he knew the magazine was not copyrighted in the United States and asked only that it be printed without change. [13]

Hubbard printed *On Going To Church* as the second Roycroft

Quarterly and edited the piece to suit himself. In fact, he offered the work as the second Roycroft Quarterly and in five hardbound book editions. Shaw's reaction is found in a letter of acknowledgment to Mrs. Richard Mansfield dated January 7, 1900.[14]

My Dear Mrs. Mansfield,
What is this?-A Roycroft book!-Have I lived-I, who let run in and out of the Kelmscott Press by William Morris-to be presented by you with the most ignorant imposture that America has yet produced? Nice of me to say this, isn't it, in return for your kindness; but I must educate you if you are to play my plays.

Listen, a few years ago, the wretch Hubbard (The Roycroft fiend) asked my permission to reprint an article of mine. I told him that as the article was not copyright, it was at his disposal or of that of any other printer in America; and that the only interest I had in the matter was that it should be honestly used-that is, printed exactly as I wrote it. On this the scoundrel proceeded to rewrite my article in his own feeble patent-medicine-advertisement English, and issued it as an "authorized edition". He then sent me two copies, with the most perfect confidence in my being pleased with his "art printing", and told me I could have some more if I wanted them. My epistolary eloquence has seldom soared so high as it did in my reply to him.

The fact is, the creature does not know the ABC of good printing. I gave him so precise an account of his ignorance in that letter that he has made some attempt to correct those which admitted of correction by mechanical instruction. For instance, he now aims at having his margins right instead of not knowing anything about them. He no longer sticks two or three fly leaves of dirty brown felt at the end, under the impression that they are "esthetic" because they are ugly and silly. He had discarded his sham "Kelmscott Capitols", the design of which would have disgraced a learned pig, and substituted colored sham Chinese ones which are much less offensive. But in the essentials of printing he is as hopeless as ever. His type is set in the stupidest commercial way. Look at a page of a Morris book, and you can see the block of letterpress constituting the printed page, as a piece of rich black on white. There are no bars of white across between the lines-no rivers of white trickling down between irregularly spaced words like drops of rain down a window pane on a wet day. You don't find half a dozen lines set sparsely and looking like a bald head, and the next half dozen squeezed into a smudge of black. The distribution of color is as beautifully even as it is in the best of old manuscripts or the early printed books which follow the rules arrived at by the manuscript scribes. The little pictures of leaves which you see occasionally in the line, which Hubbard imitates under the impression that they are mere freaks of ornament, are put in always to fill up a space which would have otherwise made a white patch on the page. Hubbard gets his type set just as an advertisement of a lost dog, or a grocer's catalogue might be set, leaving white streaks and spots all over the place, and then pops in a leaf here and there out of pure idiocy-which is what means to him. Again, look at his title page. Three different sizes of type on it! He would have got in six if he could. This is the essence of the commonest "display" work of the jobbing printer; a true artistic printer never uses two sorts of type on a page if one will do.

If you look at this simple science of printing, take a Roycroft book in one hand and a Morris book in the other. You will throw the Roycroft book out the window into its proper place, the gutter.

All this may sound needlessly fierce; but the fact is, America, having read a great deal about art, and not knowing anything about it, is being duped most frightfully by intense young people who are resolved to make Chicago flower with a fifteenth century luxuriance, and who will find one day that, as Wagner put it, they have grasped at art and let their lives slip by them.

So, no more Roycroft book ....

The Mansfield letter is the most complete vilification of Elbert Hubbard but Shaw referred to the reprinting again. In a letter to William Dana Orcutt dated August 28, 1903[15],after commenting unfavorably on the printing of one of his works by Orcutt, Shaw introduced comments and references to Roycroft such as ". . . as you have produced it, it is a perfectly shocking piece of printing-almost as bad as the work of the Roycroft shop, which is the worst in the world. He continued "If you look at one of the books printed by William Morris, the greatest printer of the XX century, and one of the greatest printers of all the centuries, you will see that he occasionally puts in a little leaf ornament, like this (illustration), or something of the kind. Your Roycroft idiots, not understanding this, pepper such things all over their 'art' books, and generally manage to stick an extra large quad before each to show how little they understand about the business." He took another jab toward the close of this letter by saying that "the Roycroft people are exhausting themselves in dirty felt and papers, sham Kelmscott capitals, leaf ornaments in quad sauce, and then wondering why nobody in Europe will pay two pence for a Roycroft book, whilst Kelmscott books and Doves Press books of Morris' friends Walker and Cobden-Sanderson fetch fancy prices before the ink is thoroughly dry."

Shaw concluded that the Roycroft people may have learned little since he last saw their work. He lamented again about the On Going To Church and commented upon the letter he sent to Hubbard (unlocated) on that occasion leaving the impression that this letter would account for any improvement in the quality of the press.

Shaw is wrong. Hubbard had no right to edit Shaw's work but Shaw knew as little about printing as Hubbard.

If Hubbard did not get Shaw's applause he certainly got his attention.

The one true literary talent that was closely associated with Elbert Hubbard and the Roycroft Press was Stephen Crane. Crane and Hubbard probably met when both were associated with the Arena Publishing Co. Stallman[16] states that B. O. Flowers of the Arena probably introduced them in 1894. Evidence indicates that Hubbard was much taken with Crane while Crane thought Hubbard with his flowing tie and cape was just another ersatz bohemian of the period. But he did enjoy Hubbard's company.

Hubbard's puritanical streak was always jarred by Crane's predilection for conversation with bums, prostitutes and others of the street and Crane later embarrassed the whole Hubbard family in East Aurora by telling his famous Negress story in their company.

When The Philistine was started Crane was one of the earliest contributors and there is at least one contribution by him in the first year's run of the magazine. Hubbard also published *A Souvenir and a Medley* by Stephen Crane as his Roycroft Quarterly No. 1.

Crane probably never offered Hubbard publication rights to any of his longer works because Hubbard would not pay royalties. It is interesting to speculate why Hubbard never approached Crane on this matter. It could be that he knew royalties would have to be paid or it could be that the ego that was to show itself throughout his own literary career would not accept a true talent as direct competition.

Nevertheless Hubbard and Crane were friendly. They corresponded up to Crane's death and most of Crane's letters to Hubbard concern Hubbard's writing. Crane thought highly of No Enemy (But Himself) and in a letter dated January 2, 1896 writes:[17]

My Dear Haich;
I read your "No Enemy" today. I always find that I better appreciate what books are to us when I wait for the moment to come when I want a book and want it badly. This afternoon I read "No Enemy" at one sitting. I like it. Your manipulation of the life in Indiana and Illinois is out of sight. There are swift character sketches all through it that strike me

as being immense. However, I sympathize with the clergyman in Chapter 1. He stated his case rather badly but he was better than Hilliard. Hilliard proved in the rest of the book that he was not what he indirectly said he was in Chapter 1.

Hilliard is a bird. Yet in Chapter 1 he was a chump. Your flower in the water-good god, that is magnificent. One thing that I felt in the roots of my hair. Hell and blazes but I do envy you that paragraph.

The book strengthened me and up-lifted me. It is a peach.

Yours Sincerely
Stephen Crane

Crane did not think much of Hubbard's Message to Garcia. [18]

Brede Place Brede Notham, Sussex May 1st, '99

My dear Hubbard:
I wrote something in '97 suggesting that you reprint in The Philistine two articles of mine which appeared in The Westminster Gazette. I have just been reading them again and I like them. I send you copies and if you are not a duffer you will consider them good and human enough for your blinding Philistine. Send me The Philistine or I will set fire to East Aurora by cable.

I have been working up some grievances against you. I object strongly to your paragraphs about Rowan. You are more wrong than is even common on our humble incompetent globe. He didn't do anything worthy at all. He received the praise of the general of the army and got to be made a lieutenant col. for a feat which about forty newspaper correspondents had already performed at the usual price of fifty dollars a week and expenses. Besides he is personally a chump and in Porto Rico where I met him he wore a yachting cap as part of his uniform which is damnable. When you want to monkey with some of our national heroes you had better ask me, because I know and your perspective is almost out of sight.

When I think of you I rejoice that there is one man in the world who can keep up a small independent monthly howler without dying, going broke, or becoming an ass.

Yours always
Stephen Crane.

Crane was also one of the targets in Hubbard's Manifesto printed in the Philistine for January, 1899. I doubt the sincerity of this whole essay.

17

Hubbard may have been somewhat serious but there is too much flippancy running throughout to afford it the maliciousness that it has been given.

Hubbard's thoughts on Crane are equally generous and in a historical perspective quite accurate.

In the *Souvenir and a Medley* Hubbard retorted to William Dean Howells criticism of *Red Badge of Courage*. "There is a class of reviewers who always wind up their preachments by saying: 'This book gives much promise, and we shall look anxiously for Mr. Scribbler's next". Let us deal in no such case. A man's work is good or it is not. As for his 'next', nobody can tell whether it will be good or not. There is a whole army of men about to do something great, but the years go by and they never do it." If Crane produced nothing more, he had already done enough "to save the fag-end of the century from literary disgrace; and like you, friends, that is no small matter!" (quoted from Smallman, pg. 183/4).

Hubbard also eulogized Crane in two obituaries. The first, printed in Feb. 1897 , after the false report of Crane's drowning in the Commodore sinking, was long and flowery and retracted in the same issue with the terse statement- "Later: Thanks to Providence and a hen coop, Steve Crane was not drowned after all-he swam ashore." It was not that simple a story but not pertinent here.

When Crane did pass away Hubbard again eulogized him. Here he started out straight but turned flowery. It is worth quoting random passages from that eulogy both as an attestation of the friendship between Crane and Hubbard and as another evidence of the one gift Elbert Hubbard had-seeing and understanding true talent. The eulogy appears in the September, 1900 Philistine and reads in part:
"Stevie is not quite at home here-he'll not remain so very long," said a woman to me in 1895. Five years have gone by, and last week the cable flashed the news that Stephen Crane was dead. Dead at twenty-nine, with ten books to his credit, two of them good, which is two more than most of us scribblers will ever write. Yes, Stephen Crane wrote two things that are immortal. "The Red Badge of Courage" is the strongest, most vivid work of the imagination ever fished from ink-pot by an American.

"Men who write from the imagination are helpless when in the presence of the fact," said James Russell Lowell. In answer to which I'll point you "The Open Boat", the sternest, creepiest bit of realism ever penned, and Stevie was in the boat.

American critics honored Stephen Crane with more ridicule, abuse and unkind comment than was bestowed on any other writer of his time. Possibly the vagueness, & the loose, unsleeked quality of his work invited the jibes, jeers and the loud laughter that tokens the vacant mind; yet as half apology for the critics we might say that scathing criticism never killed good work, and that is true, but it sometimes has killed the man.

Stephen Crane never answered back, nor made explanation, but that he was stung by the continual efforts of the press to laugh him down, I am very sure.

The lack of appreciation at home caused him to shake the dust of America from his feet and take up his abode across the sea, where his genius was being recognized, and where strong men stretched out sinewy hands of welcome, and words of appreciation were heard instead of silly, insulting parody. In passing, it is well to note that the five strongest writers of America had their passports to greatness ve-sed in England before they were granted recognition at home. I refer to Walt Whitman, Thoreau, Emerson, Poe and Stephen Crane.

Stevie did not know he cared for approbation, but his constant refusal to read what the newspapers said about him was proof that he did. He boycotted the tribe of Romeike, because he knew that nine clippings out of every ten would be unkind, and his sensitive soul shrank from the pinpricks.

Contemporary estimates are usually wrong, and Crane is only another of the long list of men of genius to whom Fame brings a wreath and finds her poet dead.-Here Hubbard starts his comparison with Chopin-then "Stephen Crane was an artist in his ability to convey the feeling by just the right word, or a word misplaced, like a lady's dress in disarray or a hat askew. This daring quality marks everything he wrote.

The recognition that language is fluid, and at best only an expedient, flavors all his work. He makes no fetish of a grammar-if the grammar gets in the way so much the worse for the grammar. All is packed with color, and charged with feeling, yet the work is usually quiet in quality and modest in manner."

Hubbard's eulogy continued but the point is that a real friendship existed between the two men.

Another writer who visited East Aurora as a friend of Elbert Hubbard was Richard LaGallienne. I don't know how they became acquainted; perhaps it was in 1900 when LaGallienne lectured on Omar Khayyham in Buffalo. Although the Roycroft Printing Shop published his *Cry of the Little Peoples* around 1903 his work did not appear in The Philistine though he is often mentioned.

Hubbard invited LaGallienne to summer at Roycroft in 1907 and this was a providential invitation for LaGallienne since he was under a physical and financial strain. He had had little success with his work published in the United States.

He lectured at Roycroft in July 1908 and again summered there in 1909. During this stay he fell victim to Hubbard's literary acquisitiveness.

LaGallienne had discussed doing "an apology for living" with Hubbard but before he could start it Hubbard had taken the idea and published it under his own name in The Philistine. LaGallienne was outraged to the point of asking Hubbard to step outside. It was LaGallienne who stepped outside and kept going. He never returned to East Aurora.[19]

LaGallienne and Crane were the only two writers of lasting prominence who were associated with Hubbard personally. All other authors of note were just his victims.

Some history of authors associated with the Roycroft Printing Shop is worth giving.

Julia Ditto Young was a Buffalo poet and wife of a prominent bank executive. She was a close friend of Elbert and Bertha and provided the first audiences for the literary Elbert at her home. The shop produced and sold her *Glynne's Wife* in 1896 and *The Story of Saville* in 1897. Some of Mrs. Youngs poetry appeared in The Philistine and she composed the Concordance and Index to the Philistine.

William McIntosh was managing editor of The Buffalo Evening News and an early contributor to The Philistine. He was also the "Doctor Phil" of the 1898 publication *Sermons from a Philistine Pulpit* and was probably closer to Harry Taber than to Elbert Hubbard. McIntosh gets a short blast in the Manifesto because of this friendship with Taber and Taber's later assertion that McIntosh was the real author of the *Message to Garcia*.[20]

Adeline Knapp was a newspaperwoman in Buffalo who was involved with the local literary circle. One of her essays appeared in The Philistine and the shop printed her *Upland Pastures* in 1897. I doubt that this was a vanity printing since the limitation statement was signed by Hubbard, not Ms. Knapp.

Ms. Knapp was sent to report on the Hawaiian revolution by the San Francisco Call and later did research on the history of the Filipino people.

Lucius Harwood Foote had a distinguished career in the U.S. Consular Service. Why his book *On The Heights* was printed by the

Roycroft shop for the California Guild of Letters is a puzzle.

Myrtle Reed was a free lance writer in New York for six years before writing *Love Letters of a Musician* in 1898. I suspect that either she knew Hubbard through their mutual publisher, G. P. Putnam, or that Putnam arranged a limited edition of her first work through Roycroft. Putnam published this same title in 1899 with great success. Today her books are collected because the covers for the Putnam editions were designed by Margaret Armstrong.

Marilla Ricker had three books published by Roycroft. All were based on her beliefs as a suffragette, free thinker and religious iconoclast. She was a lawyer who specialized in criminal law and labor reform.

Clarence Darrow was well known as a radical lawyer in Hubbard's time. He knew and liked Hubbard and spent some of his summer holidays in East Aurora. His *Persian Pearl* was first published by the Roycrofters and later reprinted by a Chicago publisher.

One of Elbert Hubbard's kindest and most constructive critics was William Marian Reedy of *Reedy's Mirror* of St. Louis. Reedy began as a reporter on the Missouri Republican and wrote independently for the weeklies. One of those weeklies was *The Sunday Mirror*, whose owner, James Campbell, made Reedy editor in 1893 and gave him the publication in 1896. Reedy used the paper to introduce new authors to his readers. Among those introduced were Edgar Lee Masters, Lord Dunsany and Joseph Conrad. I haven't found evidence of Reedy offering Hubbard space in his weekly. Whatever the circumstances of their meeting, they were good friends. Reedy enjoyed visiting East Aurora and his comments on Hubbard and his writing are probably the most astute of all of the contemporaries of Hubbard. He also left an epitaph for Hubbard: Be kind but get the mazuma (money).

THE HELP

"Be kind but get the mazuma" (money) pretty well sums up Elbert Hubbard as an employer. He couldn't tolerate competition on his home ground but there was only one condition of employment and one work rule in the early Roycroft Shops. You had to understand that Hubbard was THE BOSS and that you had to keep busy. All sources agree that as an employer Hubbard would overlook work not done quickly or correctly but would not tolerate work not done. Those who would not work were fired, or, as it was phrased at the shops, "given a one-way ticket on the four o'clock local".

The Roycroft shop became a magnet for the good, bad and indifferent in the graphic arts trade. The bad thought Hubbard didn't know what he was doing-a rich man playing at business. They were hired along with the rest but didn't last long. The good found steady employment and a chance to use their imaginations. The indifferent did what they always have done-took up space.

The good, bad and indifferent finally added up to a total weekly payroll of about 100 persons in the graphic arts areas around 1909/1910 and Hubbard had to expand his lecturing to meet the payroll.

As to the wages, we have only one ledger of 1909/1910[21] as reference. That tells us proofreaders were paid $9 a week and the head proofreader or editor, John Hoyle, received $39. Cy Rosen's salary as superintendent of the printing shop was $75 per week and other division head's salaries ranged from $24 to $40 in the non-craft areas. We will have to assume that the other creative department heads received salaries comparable to that of Mr. Rosen.

Clerks and typists were paid $5 per week and worked a 50-hour week. The beginners and unskilled workers in the shops probably received a wage comparable to the office workers. We have not been able to determine salaries for the skilled workers in the type, press and bookbinding areas, but I would guess that they were about 25% less than for comparable private industry positions.

Considering the rural cost of living and the low pressure work conditions the wages were fair and attracted competent workmen.

We mentioned the roving element of the graphic arts trades that visited Roycroft. One left a veiled description of working conditions as he found them.

Harry Kemp relates his work experiences at Eos Artwork Studios founded by one Roderick Spaltont.[22] Obviously this was the Roycroft Shops of East Aurora and Elbert Hubbard. Anyway, Kemp was given work gluing bindings and paid $3 a week and, as he puts it, "found". He tells us that the time clock was hidden from tourists by curtains and of the musical performances staged for the same tourists. The same little girl would suddenly leave her work place when there was a tour in progress and go to the piano as if suddenly inspired. We cannot corroborate Kemp but that was the theatrical effect that Hubbard appreciated. The time clock was actually hidden by a curtain and there was a piano in the illumination studio for the girls.

The shops were run on paternal lines and Elbert Hubbard took advantage of the working conditions he offered to get some free publicity. The New York State Department of Labor published the following as Employees' Welfare Institute, Monographs on Social Economics, 1904:

The Roycroft Shop
East Aurora, New York

Probably in no other industrial undertaking in the State is so much to be found that is beyond the simple payment of the stipulated wage for a certain amount of work and beyond the requirements of law with respect to the health and safety of employees, as in the Roycroft printing establishment at East Aurora. This is the natural result of the unique principle followed by the institution's founder, and still its presiding spirit, Mr. Elbert Hubbard, and which may be briefly stated as seeking the highest development of the worker by means of work under the most inspiring conditions, not only as best for the worker himself but as securing from him the best service.

The principle has been applied in a village with something less than 2,000 population, which aside from the Roycroft Shop is almost entirely an agricultural community. Except for a few skilled workmen as heads of departments and instructors, the surrounding farms have furnished all the Roycroft workers, many of whom are boys and girls, and practically all of whom were without knowledge of a trade and acquired all their skill at the work entirely within the shop. The principle has been found to be "a wise business policy", asserts Mr. Hubbard, who stated in 1902 that upon an investment of about $250,000 a net profit of over

$200,000 in seven years had been realized. One fact must be borne in mind, however, in judging of this "social and industrial experiment", as it has been called by its author. The business is chiefly artistic bookmaking and the publication of Mr. Hubbard's writings. It is, therefore, outside the field of sharp price competition, and owing to the special reputation of its founder and head enjoys a certain monopoly element in its market.

Following is a summary of the main features adopted at the Roycroft Shop in fulfillment of the principle noted above.

1. Profit sharing. The Roycroft institution was incorporated in May, 1902, under the name of The Roycrofters. The entire capital of $300,000 is owned by Roycroft workers in shares of $25 each, and no others are permitted to hold stock. Any holder quitting the employ of the company is required to sell his stock to Mr. Hubbard at the price paid for it, the latter agreeing also to pay such price. Any employee is permitted to subscribe for as many shares as he desires at par, and the stock is fully paid up, non-assessable and with no personal liability, and guaranteed to pay 12 percent dividends annually. In 1903 about one-half of the stock was owned by employees, the remainder being held by officers of the company, superintendents, etc.

2. Attractive surroundings. Exteriorly are well-kept lawns, shade trees and flower beds, which, combined with the old English style of architecture of the half dozen buildings, three of them built of stone and the location in the residence portion of the village, give the place the appearance of a school or college rather than a factory. Within, save in pressroom, carpenter and blacksmith shops, which are perforce plainer, are curtains and draperies at doors and windows, pictures and busts adorning walls or fireplace mantels, with rugs and antique furniture, more suggestive of a well-furnished library than a workshop.

3. Physical comfort of employees. Women and girls are supplied with aprons for their work. Several bathrooms, including shower, tub and a recently added Turkish bath, are at the service of the employees. In a building known as the Phalanstery is a rest room, with easy chairs, books and piano open to anyone among employees or public. Here also is a large dining room and kitchen with dormitories in the second story. A number of workers live here, receiving board in part payment of wages. Other employees who desire it are here served with meals at a charge of fifteen cents, designed to cover the actual cost only. The entire Phalanstery is for the public as well as Roycrofters, especially visitors to the institution, who are there entertained at moderate expense.

The value of physical exercise is constantly emphasized at the Roycroft Shop. Fifteen minutes per day, on the company's time, are devoted to exercise, either gymnastics indoors, under the guidance of a physical director employed by the company, or to walks outside for those who prefer, participation in the gymnastics being entirely voluntary. Tramps across country are urged at other times, and are frequently led by Mr. Hubbard or the physical director. A ball nine and an annual field day of the employees further encourage physical development, as well as a croquet ground and hand-ball court on the grounds.

4. Intellectual, aesthetic and social opportunities. Except for some studio space for art book work, the central Roycroft building is devoted entirely to these interests. One wing constitutes the "chapel", as it is called, where as a rule on Saturday and Sunday evenings and frequently at other times, concerts, lectures or talks are given either by someone connected with the institution, or often by talent from abroad, including many notables. The chapel is at the same time an art gallery, with walls covered with paintings largely the work of the Roycrofters' own artists.

In the tower room of the chapel on the first floor is a small library of books, many of them the Roycroft product. In the second story are rooms where evening classes are held, all open to employees without expense save that each must purchase his own books. All the instructors are workers in the shop and there are classes in modern languages, literature, history, designing, etc., with exercises in debating. A special feature is made of music, in charge of a musical director from outside.

Instruction in voice and piano is offered employees free, and those who undertake such study are permitted to take a half-hour daily in working time for practice or lessons. Besides pianos in the Phalanstery and chapel, there are two others in the main work building, all for the use of employees and frequently utilized in recreation hours for dancing. A band, glee and mandolin clubs are maintained among the employees, the company having paid one-half the cost of instruments and advanced the other half to be paid back out of the proceeds of concerts.

Clubroom facilities and place for social intercourse abound at the Roycroft Shop. All the buildings are open at all times and employees are encouraged to use them freely. The large reception hall in the chapel building for larger gatherings and the Phalanstery restroom and many of the workrooms are attractive for smaller social meetings. It is the constant aim, in fact, to cultivate the feeling that the Roycroft Shop is for the workers, not simply as a workplace where a living may be earned, but as a center for recreation, culture and social.

Although this is taken from the Roycrofters' own publications it is true. The profit sharing idea didn't last long, but Hubbard had his own bank on the premises and workers were encouraged to deposit some of their wages every week.

The Roycroft campus was an enjoyable place to work, especially considering the general working conditions around the country at the time. How many young people in a rural village could return to their workplace in the evenings and on weekends to hear Eugene Debs, Carrie Jacobs Bond, Gutzon Borglum, Harry Lauder, Margaret Sanger, John Burroughs, Clarence Darrow, Booker T. Washington, etc.? The employees of those early days could meet the famous and infamous. They enjoyed the visitors and many interviewed recall secretly enjoying the grumbling of their neighbors about the terrible people Elbert Hubbard brought to their village.

These employees interviewed unanimously praised Elbert Hubbard for his concern for them. They did enjoy exercise breaks, free lectures and were not overworked. The girls were assigned to the bindery, mail room or office. Those who took the free art classes and showed some ability were sent to the illumination studio to work on the hand decorated books. There those who showed above average drawing skill were given the illustration work while the other girls would fill in printed outlines with water colors.

A young man would be sent into the shop he preferred if there was an immediate opening or put on a waiting list if the shop foreman was agreeable to his future employment. Training was competent as evidenced by the general quality achieved in the shop's output. These were local people in a farm area and one must applaud the results of their serious efforts.

The daughters of Cy Rosen have pleasant memories of their youths spent at Roycroft. They were often conscripted as tour guides and recall the generally relaxed atmosphere and their father's pleasure in his work until Alice Moore Hubbard took over the print shop. Their brother is an illustration of the benevolent nepotism of the shop. Elbert Hubbard Rosen was a Monotype operator in the type area of the shop.[23]

Mrs. Hugh Williamson also recalls Roycroft fondly. She left high school in her third year, started in the mail room and was promoted to proofreading with John Hoyle. She relates one incident concerning Alice Hubbard. She delivered a catalog proof to Alice for approval. Mrs. Hubbard approved the copy but hesitated returning the proof. Mrs. Williamson correctly guessed that Alice could not remember her name and she volunteered "Hazel" to which Alice replied:"I thought of every

26

other nut!" Mrs. Williamson also corroborates the recreational and educational opportunities noted in the Labor Department report.[24]

Mrs. Belle Knight's entire family worked at Roycroft. She started part-time addressing envelopes at $2.00 per thousand after school and then was Cy Rosen's secretary from 1915 to 1918. She was Bert Hubbard's secretary from 1924 until the shops closed. Mrs. Knight also remembers her employment at Roycroft fondly. She summed up the attitude as "no pressure and freedom from strict supervision as long as we were working."[25]

Merritt Keyser worked as an illuminator for four years. In an undated newspaper clipping found in the Aurora Historical Society archives he describes his work experience at Roycroft. He tells us that there were about twenty-five illuminators and illustrators and that Hubbard would often drop into the studio and invite all out for a walk. If the walk went on for a bit Hubbard would remark that it took more time than he expected and everyone might as well take the rest of the day off. Keyser noted that this won loyalty-and boosted production when work did resume. When Hubbard heard that Keyser was a musician he made arrangements for him to study with the resident music instructor at Roycroft. Later Keyser was head of the Roycroft band and Hubbard would come to band practices at the power plant. He goes on to relate how Hubbard lent him a new car for his honeymoon and then told Keyser to keep the car for the rest of the summer since none of the other employees knew how to care for it.

Keyser had to give up illuminating because of declining eyesight but his musical education at Roycroft led him to a second and longer career as a musician in Buffalo.

Emil Georg Sahlin[26] recalled that when Hubbard was annoyed with the help he posted signs describing the infraction of rules and warned that he did not expect a repetition. If Alice were around, however, things were different. Sahlin corroborated Alice Moore Hubbard's no-nonsense attitude in the shop. He tells us that in his time (1913-1915) one of the first casualties of the start of the decline of the enterprise was the Christmas bonus. Elbert had been in the habit of giving $5.00 gold pieces or Howard watches to regular employees. Alice changed that to a pair of woolen mittens. Emil had followed his brother Axel into the Roycroft Shop. Both were typographers and both enjoyed their years there according to Emil's recollections. Then they both had long and successful careers in typography in Buffalo. Emil also noted that experimentation was encouraged and his brother Axel turned out some very nice bookbindings.

Ernest Simmons[27] also related how the shops changed when Alice took over. He was Elbert's secretary and recalled one memo sent to him. He was, in the future, to send all lecture cards and announcements in one cent envelopes and he was to watch the returns on all sales solicitations. Any mailing that did not return at least ten percent was to be discontinued at once. She signed this note with Elbert's initials. Alice also decided that all wages were to be figured by the hourly rate down to the smallest fraction of time so employees would get paid for the exact time they worked. This communication was sent over Bert's signature.

Alice Hubbard brought a different atmosphere to the shop. We do have another account of life at Roycroft that shows it in a different light.

Robert Lane was sent east from Corvallis, Oregon to East Aurora in 1913. He had been enrolled in "The Roycroft School of Life"-another Elbert Hubbard money-maker. His mother paid $125.00 for tuition, room, board and a semester of education and craft training. No matter what "The Roycroft School of Life" was supposed to be, Mr. Lane tells us what it really was like from January to June 1913.

There were eleven boys and two girls in his class and the headmistress was a Mrs. Atwood. The school routine was to be up early, breakfast on one shredded wheat biscuit and a then morning of class work. On clement days Elbert Hubbard would show up about one o'clock to "go for a walk" that always ended at the farm manure pile where pitch forks would be waiting. The pile was pitched until sunset and then they walked back to Emerson Hall.

Lane was puzzled why his mother had paid for practical experience, printing in his case, and all he ever saw was the manure pile. After a talk about bookbinding by Alice Hubbard, he cornered her and asked to be put in the printing shop and to be paid for his work. Part of the puzzlement about the manure pile was that they knew that he could operate a Model 8 Linotype and was familiar with printing processes in general. He does not tell us his family background in Oregon but writes throughout his correspondence with such surety that his account can't really be questioned.

He got the job in the shop, fifty-four hours a week was the standard and whatever he did beyond that would bring seven cents an hour. He found little encouragement to learn more about the graphic arts but did show his worth in typesetting, making corrections and feeding the job presses. He started to return to the shop at night to experiment with the equipment on his own but when Alice found out he was dismissed from the shop. That started a period of conflict between Lane and Alice. He ran away twice and wrote his mother imploring her to bring him back to Oregon. The whole East Aurora operation was a sham as far as he was concerned. They had taken his mother's money and were giving nothing of value in return.

He finally made it to his grandparents' farm in Lounsberry, New York and that ended his six month or so association with Roycroft. He never found Alice maternal, friendly or helpful. He stated that her daughter Miriam was liked by all but that Elbert Hubbard II (Bert) was remote and closemouthed.

This account may seem rather precise for a memory of many years past but the drawings accompanying his notes precisely place every piece of equipment in the shop by name and is accurate by our own investigation. [28]

I wish we had more personal histories of the average worker at Roycroft but too much time has passed. Those who gained prominence or remained in the graphic arts after their association with Roycroft were more easily documented.

Those in creative or supervisory positions found the Roycroft shop a good stepping stone to better positions or prominence. All of the evidence now on hand shows that the creative personnel and administrators noted below left the shop for better positions or to establish themselves independently.

W. W. Denslow wrote to Hubbard in 1896 requesting a copy of the *Song of Songs* and, according to habit, decorated the letter with marginal drawings. These attracted Hubbard and he enclosed a note with the book inquiring on Denslow's availability and interest in decorating Roycroft books. The second round of correspondence got down to business. Denslow's note[29] offers his services:

Early Candlelight,
The Studio by the Lake,
Highwood, Ill.
July 20th, 1896

Mr. Elbert Hubbard,
Dear Friend and Fellow Philistine,
I thank you much for the portrait. It shall have the place of honor in my

studio by the lake. It is not near the salt water such as you have at Hell
Gate. But it is the best we can do out here.
I have often wished that you would use illustrations in The Philistine
as, then, I might hope to, some day, become a contributor.
>   Yours very truly,
>   W. W. Denslow

Hubbard's reply is tongue-in-cheek as usual.

>   East Aurora, N.Y.
>   Aug. 14, 1896

Dear Mr. Denslow,

Let me state the assuring fact that this village is 400 miles from Hell
Gate. It is 18 miles So. East from Buffalo on the "Philadelphia" road. It
has 200 inhabitants, 6 churches, the same number of saloons, and a first
class graded school.

  I have one wife, three boys and a daughter. My oldest boy is 13, the
daughter seven months. We keep one hired girl, one cow, a pony and
100 chickens. My wife keeps my accts., opens and answers most of my
correspondence and takes care of my money. She is not a literary woman
and is not so awful damn smart, but you can guess that she is a great
help to me. We have not paid a dollar doctor bill in five years, for the
peculiar reason that we have had no doctor to visit us, not even when
the baby was born. I wear old shoes, corduroy trousers and a hat. It costs
us about one thousand a year to live. We have kind neighbors, but few
of them are bookish, and none to speak of artistic, and The Philistine is
an enigma to all but three.

  Yet, I have a following scattered all over the earth,-not large but a few
people who say: Record my order for a copy of everything you write or
print. A few of these people are rich, and our vellum paper books @ $5.00
have sold first, and I now see that a book with a dash of hand color in it
is prized. How much in dollars I do not know. People buy hand painted
china, hand painted vases, and pay a hundred dollars a piece; will they
do so for books? I do not know.

  Our little printing shop works only two men and two women. It is a
tuppenny affair, but we can print beautiful books. The soft (Holland)
paper used in The Song of Songs is not right for decorating but vellum
paper is and genuine vellum is better still. I am going to reprint the
enclosed Goldsmith essay on Japanese vellum-breaking the text up into
chapters, then leaving large open spaces that can be filled in. This will

give the artist a chance. Then I'm going to make up a list of our choicest customers and find out how much they will pay for a beautiful book.

There is no competition in this line, for the reason there is no demand. It is a virgin field. Now having spied out the land, can you and I go in and possess it? Do you want to cast your lot and couple your name with the Roycroft? Of course, if you make a success of it, others will follow, but we must keep free of competition by doing a better work than the imitators-we must hold our pose as the Great and Only.

What will you charge me for coming on here and working a month? In that time, we can get acquainted with each other, and with the business, too. If there is a field here we should have sense enough to work side by side for a mutual advantage and benefit.

Denslow's first work for Hubbard was illustrating twelve copies of the *Art and Life*. Hubbard probably sent unbound sheets to Denslow in Chicago because Denslow did not visit East Aurora until the spring of 1898. There he took over the back cover of the Philistine and produced cartoons that had a bite equal to the best of Beerbohm or Beardsley in his private letters. Stephen Crane was a favorite target and Denslow invented the character of "Ali Baba" based on Hubbard's handyman Anson Blackman. One of the cartoons was enlarged to a poster titled "Books to Burn".

Denslow also designed bindings, initial letters and title pages for the regular and limited editions. His work for the press included: *Art and Life*, 1896; *Ruskin-Turner*, 1896; *Love Ballads of the XVIth Century*, 1897; *Sesame and Lilies*, 1897; *As It Seems To Me*, 1898; *The Dipsy Chanty*, 1898; *Ballads of a Book Worm*, 1898; *The Deserted Village*, 1898; *Sonnets from the Portuguese*, 1898; *Confessions of an Opium Eater*, 1898; *Rime of the Ancient Mariner*, 1899 and his designs are seen in four Rubaiyats.

His work is easily identified by his mark-the seahorse. He was called "Hippocampus Den" around the Roycroft shop and his seahorse mark was incorporated into the Roycroft water mark and signed all of his contributions to the press and its publications.

Denslow returned to East Aurora in 1899 with his wife and Laurence Mazanovich, a young artist friend from Chicago for a short visit. He did not return to East Aurora again. He had just finished the illustrations for the first of his friend L. Frank Baum's books about a place called Oz. Denslow would not need East Aurora after he found Oz.

An examination of the work Denslow did for Roycroft shows his best work were the cartoons and caricatures done for the Philistine. His book designs are quite weak and show a lack of understanding of good book design and of developing the book as a unit. Of course, there was no one at East Aurora to offer guidance beyond the technical aspects of book production. Another young man who came to East Aurora used Roycroft as his school-but he was his own teacher.

Dard Hunter's reputation rests with his work on the history of paper and papermaking. His best work as a graphic designer was done during his years at Roycroft.

Hunter ended up in East Aurora because he was affected by the work of the Kelmscott Press and sought a sympathetic educational opportunity in the United States. His only lead to his goal was his brother's copies of The Philistine. Believing that the Society of the Philistines and the Roycroft Printing Shop were true exponents of the arts and crafts movement philosophy, he wrote to Hubbard asking for employment. Hubbard returned a polite but negative letter which did not deter Hunter. He left Ohio for East Aurora to apply for work in person. He arrived in 1903 and he stayed until 1910 with some brief separations. He did not arrive without some knowledge since his father and brother were newspapermen and the senior Hunter had a private press. Hubbard decided to give Hunter a chance at designing rather than putting him into one of the shops but he would would have to find his own way.

He saw that the library at Roycroft had two or three incunabula, some art books, runs of International Studio and one or two Kelmscotts. This would be his source material when he started to draw the initial letters for the limited editions.

Hunter gives us another example of the complex personality of Elbert Hubbard. Standard Oil commissioned Hubbard to write a preachment as part of their campaign to dispel or offset the ill-will generated by the popular press that likened the oil monopoly to an octopus. Hunter was given the assignment to design a cover and sketched out a very stylized octopus (figure 1). When he showed the proposed cover to Hubbard he did not realize the gravity of the situation. Standard Oil was a huge corporation that was willing to pay well and John D. Rockefeller was a friend of Hubbard. The Fra looked at the design and Hunter began to have misgivings about his brashness. Finally Hubbard handed the sketch back to Hunter and said "that's great, the officials of the oil company are so imbued with their own self-righteousness they'll never recognize themselves." The brown and black pamphlet with the stylized octopus motif was printed and distributed by the thousands, but the oil company never discovered nor admitted seeing the hidden message.[30]

Hunter left the shops in 1908 to study in Europe. He returned later, worked in his old design studio and then left for good. His subsequent career in printing and the history of paper making marks him as one of the greats in graphic arts history.

It is interesting to speculate what or where Dard Hunter would have ended up if he had not started at the Roycroft shops. I have no doubts that he would have pursued the same career. If he had studied in Europe and not worked at the Roycroft shop he might have attained a level of aesthetic and creative maturity sooner but I don't think Roycroft hurt him. What he lost in creative challenge he gained in the freedom to experiment and to set and evaluate his own goals as a designer. It is true that much of his design work done at Roycroft is derivative but much work done by young artists and designers is derivative until they achieve some confidence in their own abilities. That confidence is gained by experimentation and Roycroft was the best place at the time for the young creative mind. Hunter's work in metal, glass, and the myriad experiences in graphics encompassing everything from books to calendars to advertisements could only be duplicated today, seventy some years later, in a four year professional design school. He lacked only the supervision and guidance of experienced designers, but he still succeeded. Hunter later claimed that he learned nothing at Roycroft but that claim was either in relation to his later work as a historian or he was trying to disassociate himself from Hubbard.

He did learn much in East Aurora, and if his graphic design efforts did not further his career as a designer they gave him an opportunity to learn to choose and to organize his materials; extremely valuable assets in any profession.

One member of the Roycroft shops who could have had a great teaching influence upon Hunter if he had chosen to work in the binding area was Louis H. Kinder.

Kinder joined the Roycroft print shop in 1896 when he was twenty-nine and worked there with some slight interruptions for sixteen years.[31] He established a first class hand bindery, a large mechanical bindery and trained several young men who later established themselves as proficient hand binders. During his years at Roycroft Kinder apparently had a unique business relationship with Hubbard. His *Formula for Bookbinders* was printed on the Roycroft presses but was jointly published by Roycroft and G. P. Putnam's Sons. In his foreword Kinder thanks Hubbard in the past tense for all of his support. A cancel over the 1904 of the 1904/1905 copyright indicated that Kinder may have completed the manuscript while he was away from Roycroft in 1903. In that year, he, A. A. Andrews and the printing writer George French had a fling at fine printing by establishing the Imperial Press in Cleveland. The success of that venture can be gauged by the notice in The Aurora Advertiser of March 1904 noting that the Kinder family had returned to East Aurora and Mr. Kinder had assumed his former position at the Roycroft Bindery.

Many questions about the relationship between Kinder and Elbert Hubbard have been answered by a series of letters between Elbert Hubbard and Lyman Chandler.[32] These letters reinforce the other circumstantial evidence that although Kinder and Hubbard respected each other's abilities, they could not agree on how the bindery should be run. Kinder was an old school craftsman who did things "right" while Hubbard saw the bindery as part of the whole enterprise and an area that had to make money. These letters also tell us the feelings between Kinder and Hubbard regarding the publishing of The Whisper and Formula for Bookbinders. Hubbard knew that Kinder lacked the business sense and money to handle the projects and he also knew that Kinder would get hurt by the lack of acceptance for The Whisper. Kinder should have accepted his role at Roycroft. It was unique and he would never find its equal for self-expression as a binder.

Another venture that Kinder shared in was the Roycroft School of Bookbinding. This was one of Hubbard's schemes that really provided the shops with a pool of labor trained to work in the shops at the expense of the trainee. I don't know if Kinder saw any of the tuition money for overseeing these young workers but I have a feeling based on the other evidence that there was some sharing of money.

Kinder left Roycroft for good in 1912 and established a commercial bindery with Clifford Bunce in Buffalo. After 1914 we lose track of Kinder until he reappears in the Avena Shop in Chautauqua, New York in 1927.[33]

We know that he did considerable work for William Edwin Rudge before establishing the bindery at Baker Library of Dartmouth College in 1933 and working in that bindery until his death in 1938.[34]

Kinder's bindings at Roycroft are unsigned. They can usually be identified by their moderate but excellently done decoration and beautiful jeweling. He favored the thin English straw boards and that can be an identifier of a Kinder binding.

Among those attracted to or trained at Roycroft were Lorenz Schwartz, Harry Avery, Peter Frank, Axel Sahlin, Sterling Lord, John Grabau and the Younger brothers, Charles and Peter.

Lorenz Schwartz came from Germany in 1904 at the age of 28 and had worked as superintendent and designer at the Otto Zahn Bindery in Tennessee. He left after the death of the Hubbards but later returned. His work is identified with the imprinted L over S monogram.

The bindings of Avery, Frank and Lord do not have strong associations with the Roycroft shop. Axel Sahlin was a typographer whose bindings are identified with the AS monogram.

John Grabau started at the Roycroft bindery in 1902 and was later appointed assistant head of the shop. A catalog of an exhibition of his bindings at the Albright-Knox Art Gallery in Buffalo in December 1930 commemorated his twenty-fifth year in bookbinding but most of his work was done after he left Roycroft in 1915(?). It is good work in general but lacks the tooling and jeweling finesse of Kinder's work.

Charles and Peter Younger were trained by Kinder and Charles succeeded Kinder as head of the bindery in 1912. His bindings are just signed Roycroft and are quite ordinary. Peter Younger was also just an ordinary binder.

As Kinder came in to run a bindery, the first employee of the printing shop was brought in to run the printing shop.

Charles "Cy" Rosen was superintendent of the printing shop for most of its existence. He was born in Sweden and came to the United States when he was nine. He left home because of family problems when he was twelve and found work in print shops as an apprentice. When he was twenty-five years old and employed as a journeyman printer in Cherry Creek, New York he wrote to White and Wagoner in East Aurora asking about a position.[35] They replied with an offer and he moved to East Aurora. He arrived in late April 1896 and was married there in October of the same year.

When Elbert Hubbard bought out Harry Taber and removed the equipment from White and Wagoner's premises he asked Cy Rosen to come along. Rosen obviously found the possibilities interesting with Hubbard. He may have had some part in the first two Roycroft books done at White and Wagoner's but more than likely he was responsible for the job printing that kept the small printers/publishers going.

Cy Rosen developed the Roycroft printing shop. It had to be his knowledge and organizational skills that brought the shop from a one man operation to one of the largest general printing shops in the Eastern United States. He also instilled the high craft standards that made the Roycroft graphic products as well printed as any other printed material available in the United States at the time.

He left the Roycroft shop in 1912 because of differences with Alice Hubbard. She started to cut corners in the production of the books without consultation and instituted work rules that Rosen felt were unwarranted. Since Alice was the dominant force in the print shop with the blessing of Elbert Hubbard it was Cy Rosen who left. He went to work for a Niagara Falls newspaper and when he returned home to East Aurora on weekends he and Hubbard would walk the railroad tracks and talk, a sign of the friendship of Rosen and Hubbard and of the domineering influence of Alice Hubbard.

Rosen was working in Cleveland when Alice and Elbert Hubbard died. He was called to East Aurora for the reading of the wills he had once witnessed and at that time Elbert Hubbard II asked him to return as superintendent of the printing shop. He did return and remained with the shop until 1935. One Saturday he found a note on his desk informing him that he was through. It was a very unkind thank you to a man who had put the shop together and kept it together through its growth and decline.³⁶

There were others noted in Roycroft books that made solid contributions to the success of the press.

A. V. Ingham, whose name appears in several colophons, apparently was Cy Rosen's replacement. "Ing" came from Chicago and was experienced as a plant supervisor. There is little information on the man though he was apparently on the payroll before taking over for Rosen in 1912. Whether he remained on the payroll after Rosen's return in 1915 is unknown.

Alex Fournier was the art director of the printing shop with some reputation as a painter.

John Hoyle was editor-in-chief of the shop. Proofreading was his primary responsibility and the error free copy found in the Roycroft books is a tribute to him.

Samuel Warner was touted by Elbert Hubbard as London trained and a "Fellow of the Royal Society of Artists". There is no record of a "Royal Society of Artists" and Warner was from Scranton, Pennsylvania. He did study at the National Academy of Design in New York and he did bring professional experience to East Aurora when he set up the illumination studio in 1899. He taught the locals to draw and use water colors in the studio and in the various "schools" set up as talent pools. His own work at Roycroft is totally derivative from contemporary sources available in the Roycroft library. He left East Aurora in 1903 and until recently nothing more was known of Warner until Charles Hamilton, the Roycroft historian and writer met Warner's son in Florida and filled in the missing years. According to Hamilton in a program accompanying an exhibition of Warner's work, Warner went to the Boston area after his Roycroft years where he taught and developed art programs for the local school systems.[37]

A. R. Andrews was another early Roycroft employee who left no tracks after his East Aurora days. He was foreman of the job printing department of the Batavia, New York Daily News when he wrote an article describing the Roycroft shop for The American Printer in 1900. This article led to a job at the Roycroft shop as a foreman. He left in 1903 with Kinder to form the Imperial Press mentioned earlier. We have no further record of Andrews after 1903.

Jules Maurice Gaspard did most of the illustrations for the Little Journeys. We have no evidence that he lived for any time in East Aurora or was considered an employee though Dard Hunter compiled a list of those who worked with him between 1903-1909 and Gaspard's name is given. We do know that Roycroft purchased the tipped-in engravings from New York before and after setting up their own engraving shop in the bindery tower. Gaspard was Director of The Chicago Inter-Ocean art department before his association with Roycroft.

Raymond Nott joined the Roycroft shop in 1904 and stayed until 1916. He did quite a bit of work on the books and especially in the book plate business that was offered. His work is not exceptional and nothing has been learned of his career after Roycroft.

There is little information on others associated with the shop. Most were local people who did not have careers beyond East Aurora.

Whatever their backgrounds or talents they all found employment in what has to be one of the more interesting printing establishments in this country.

They were part of an idea that started with one man and went to over five hundred employees in all the Roycroft shops and services in a little more than ten years.

It was an excellent training ground for beginning artist and craftsmen and gave experienced craftsmen an opportunity to work creatively in a pleasant work environment. All interviewed who had worked there or had parents who had worked at Roycroft spoke of the satisfaction of employment in the shops.

Harry P. Taber, Founder of the Roycroft Printing Shop

THE PRINTING SHOP
The true beginning of the Roycroft printing shop is as confusing as anything else touched by Elbert Hubbard. It was a Roycroft legend that
Hubbard was inspired by his visit to William Morris and his conversation with Morris that led to the Roycroft Printing Shop. This is pure legend.

According to Elbert Hubbard ll. in his *Impressions*[38] he and his father
visited Morris' Hammersmith residence and shop on Tuesday, June 30,
1896. William Cockerell, Morris' secretary, gave them a tour and
Douglas Cockerell, bookbinding pupil of T. J. Cobden-Sanderson,
showed them the Chaucer sheets. William Morris was ill and did not
receive the Hubbards. Hubbard also declined to reserve a copy of the
Chaucer because he thought it was overpriced. This was the only time
that Hubbard and William Morris ever came close to meeting and if the
visit to Hammersmith did give Hubbard the encouragement to start fine
printing, it did not lead to the establishment of the Roycroft Printing
Shop.

The Roycroft Printing Shop was founded by Harry P. Taber. Hubbard
met Harry Taber through the Larkin Company. Taber was a salesman
for the lithographic printing firm of Cusack and Company of Buffalo
and the Larkin Company was one of Cusack's customers. Taber handled
this account when Hubbard was still Advertising Manager and they
worked together on several promotions. One of these promotions is
worth noting. It was an album of pictures and biographical sketches of
authors, something quite similar to the later Little Journeys.

Taber went to Denver in 1890 but returned to East Aurora in 1893 with
the idea for The Philistine. In an unpublished account[39] he states that he
purchased an interest in White and Wagoner's Pendennis Press.
Hubbard approached him and asked his help in preparing a new novel.
The book would be illustrated photographically using Hubbard's
friends and neighbors. The book was published and Taber's photo
appears illustrating the hero in Hubbard's *No Enemy*.

In 1895 Hubbard planned a tour of Europe and to write a book of his
experiences. Taber counter-proposed a journal recording the lives of

famous European authors and he noted the trip in his column of the Pendennis Press' *The Citizen* as a "little journey to the homes of great men." Hubbard took Taber's advice and on returning sent the manuscript on the rounds of commercial publishers. It was not accepted. At that point Taber suggested that they prepare sample copies of the little journey similar to those done by printers and advertising agencies soliciting work. Hubbard agreed and they set up the type and printed copies using a different publisher's imprint on each completed copy. G. P. Putnam's Sons then accepted the idea and contracted with Hubbard to write a little journey a month.

With Elbert Hubbard set up Taber turned to his own idea. He and his Denver friends had enjoyed the little magazines of the time and now that he had access to printing equipment he would do his own.

He published The Philistine in June 1895 in an edition of 2500 copies. The magazine would not bring in enough to support him but he hoped that it might continue long enough to attract some good advertising and pay for itself. He also started setting up the first book of the Roycroft Printing Shop. He had chosen this name by chance. While he was setting up his small operation he had seen some promotional material from American Type Founders on their new Roycroft type face. The name itself commemorated the Roycroft brothers of sixteenth century England. He adopted the name and joined it with the mark, with alterations, of Nicolas Jenson, the early Venetian printer. He describes the selection of the symbol in a letter dated June 24, 1948.[40] The letter was written to refute Hubbard's claim of invention. He wrote:

I have read with much interest-not unmixed with amazement-the article in the East Aurora Advertiser of May 13, 1948, concerning what is described as "The Hubbard Symbol". Unfortunately I was not present at the building of the pyramids at Gizen, so I cannot speak with authority as to the use of this device among the carvings found by delvers into tombs of ancient monarchs, its significance or its meaning. The learned author of The Advertiser's story quotes Elbert Hubbard as having said that he first used the familiar Roycroft trademark in June, 1895, and that the double cross "is a Dagonic device". If this reporter's memory serves, Dagon was the chief idol of the Philistines and was usually represented as half man and half fish. This leads us to the not unreasonable supposition that Dagon was the inventor of the fish story. This double cross, or Dagonic sign, may therefore, be considered as emblematic of the Tall Story or Munchausen-like tale of the fish that got away. There is no necessity for entering here into a discussion of the generally accepted meaning of the double cross.

The unidentified writer of the article in question quotes Elbert Hubbard as saying that he used the Roycroft symbol first in June 1895. This statement is in error. The device was first used on the title page of The Song of Songs-a reprint of the bible story together with a study by Elbert Hubbard. This book was designed and hand-printed by myself, as anyone may read in the colophon affixed to the original edition. I am told that in further editions my name was omitted from the colophon-a gratuitous gesture over which I am not unduly pained.

The Roycroft trademark was adapted from a similar emblem found in a book of Printer's Marks published by Scribners about 1894. I deliberately cribbed this, inserting the letter R in the lower hemisphere of the circle, had it engraved and used it as the Roycroft device in the book above mentioned. The first sheet containing the emblem was printed in September 1895. Elbert Hubbard did not come into possession of the Roycroft Shop until November 29, 1895. The original contract of sale is on my desk at this moment and a photographic copy may be found together with other highly entertaining Hubbardiana in Grosvenor Library[41] in Buffalo. Obviously, therefore, as the Roycroft trademark did not exist as such until September 1895, Hubbard could not have used it in June of that year. The frantic search for the meaning of the symbol is amusing. When, fifty-two years ago I adopted it as a printer's mark for my Roycroft Shop, I hesitated for a considerable time in my choice. There were many interesting devices available. I wanted something distinctive and it finally came to a toss-up between the one chosen and that used by William Caxton in the printed Golden Legend of 1484. If I had taken the Caxton mark it might have occasioned more controversy even than has the one under discussion; it is too cryptic, and only one versed in the typography of the fifteenth century could possibly decipher it.

However, that is beside the point. What I mean to make definitely clear is that Elbert Hubbard had nothing whatever to do with the choosing of the Roycroft emblem nor with the naming of the Roycroft Shop. Both these endeavors were my own and were sold to Elbert Hubbard as above noted on November 29, 1895. The speculations of the writer of The Advertiser's article concerning the origin of the Roycroft symbol may be interesting as studies in Egyptology and the statement of Elbert Hubbard ll to the effect that the circle is symbolic of Roycroft endeavor is at least complimentary to the one who chose it as a trademark by chance over the cryptic Caxton device.

Just one more item: David Balch in his biography[42] of Hubbard says that some people believe that the person whom he calls "The Tabers'

boy, Harry" was responsible for the beginnings of "Little Journeys".
Anyone who can get up courage enough and has sufficient interest to
examine the copy of the first edition of these essays in the Grosvenor
Library may find this inscription on its flyleaf: "To H. P. Taber, on whose
head be the blame for the existence of this book, having first suggested
it . . " This inscription is in the handwriting of Elbert Hubbard, and is
signed "E. H.".
What price glory!

To continue this debate of the invention of the Roycroft mark we look
to a 1927 Roycroft catalog. It repeats Hubbard's tale of the invention of
the mark. It states: "The Roycroft trademark (registered) is an adapta-
tion of the signum of Cassiodorus, a Benedictine monk. The circle rep-
resents unity and the cross sincere religious duty and privilege. The
mark was placed by him at the end of his beautifully illuminated manuscript. The Roycrofters added the R. They use the mark in much the
same spirit that enthused Cassiodorus. "
This piece of nonsense and Taber's believable evidence give Harry P.
Taber the credit for starting The Roycroft Printing Shop and designing
its device. The following confirms his printing and publishing the first
book issued by the press. It is the colophon of *The Song of Songs*.

AND HERE, THEN, IS FINISHED THIS NOBLE BOOK, BEING A
STUDY BY ELBERT HUBBARD AND A REPRINT OF THE SONG OF
SONGS: WHICH IS SOLOMON'S, TAKEN FROM THE HOLY BIBLE.
PRINTED AFTER THE MANNER OF THE VENETIANS WITH NO
POWER SAVE THAT OF HUMAN MUSCLE BY HARRY P. TABER, AT
THE ROYCROFT PRINTING SHOP, THAT IS IN EAST AURORA, NEW
YORK, BEGUN ON SEPTEMBER THE THIRD DAY, MDCCCXCV, AND
FINISHED-THANK GOD!-ON JANUARY THE TWENTIETH DAY,
MDCCCXCVI.

The colophon tells the early history of the shop. Taber began the book
in September and finished it in January. He started it on his own press
in his own shop and finished it on Elbert Hubbard's press in Elbert
Hubbard's shop
Why did Taber have to sell out to Hubbard? Because he simply could
not afford to run the shop. The Philistine was not selling and Taber's
investment in the Pendennis Press was proving a poor investment.
Elbert Hubbard had the money and interest in continuing the enterprise

so Elbert Hubbard became the owner. The contract referred to in Taber's
statement of rebuttal noted earlier provided that:

1. For a good and valuable consideration Mr. Taber hereby transfers all
his rights, title and interest in Roycroft Printing Shop to Mr. Hubbard. 2.
Mr. Taber agrees to devote all his time to the business and conducting
the Roycroft Printing Shop and The Philistine magazine, for which service he is to receive from Mr. Hubbard the sum of (blacked out on contract) per week, payable weekly. 3. Mr. Hubbard further agrees to pay
over to Mr. Taber semi-annually on each Jan. 1st and July 1st one-half of
all net profits on The Philistine magazine and the Roycroft Printing
Shop, first deducting the wages already paid to Mr. Taber.[43]

This agreement did not last. Various correspondence left by Taber in
the archives in Buffalo tell of his attempt to repurchase the shop soon
after this agreement. He claims, though there is no evidence to support
his claim, that Hubbard agreed to sell out for seventy-five hundred dollars and Eugene White of the Pendennis Press went to New York to buy
new equipment and type. There he supposedly met Stephen Crane and
agreed to publish Crane's next book. When they returned to East Aurora
Hubbard informed Taber that he had changed his mind and would not
sell. At this point Taber canceled the New York orders and became the
associate editor of The Buffalo Evening News.[44] All of this cannot be true.
If Taber did have seventy-five hundred dollars he would not have had
to sell out. This is just the bitterness of Taber towards Hubbard for the
latter's success. Taber did start the Roycroft Printing Shop and The
Philistine and that credit is his but none of the success of the press can
be credited to him. Elbert Hubbard can claim that credit.

Hubbard started the second book issued by the press, *The Journal of
Koheleth* ,in the shop's original location at the Pendennis Press in the
Regulator Building on Main Street. White and Wagoner's financial trou-
bles worsened and they sold *The Citizen* on September 17,1896 and then
Wagoner sold his interest in the printing shop to White on October 8,
1896. At this point Hubbard purchased some or all of their equipment.

An account given in Dirlam/Simmons *Sinners, This is East Aurora*
states that there were two small presses with two men and a boy to operate them. One of the two men or boys was Cy Rosen and Hubbard got
him along with the cases of ATF Satanick and Old Style Antique. The

Washington press that became the type shop proof press also came along in the deal. Other accounts mention[45]a flat-bed press and two stitchers that Hubbard stored for the time being. I don't know if the flat-bed press was ever used. Whatever they had to work with stayed in the Regulator Building until Hubbard had his own shop constructed on his own property on South Grove Street. Ground was broken on October 14, 1896 and the building was occupied on January 20, 1897. The presses were put in the basement; type cases, binding and shipping were on the first floor and the illuminator's studio was on the second floor.

The third book issued by the press, *Art and Life*, was the first book done in the new shop. This book tells us that Cy Rosen had taken over the shop, as it is a great improvement over the first two books. The paper stock choice, better inking plus a decent binding show the mark of a trained graphic artisan. Bertha Hubbard, who had done the illumination for the first two books, was replaced by Samuel Warner. Warner set up the studio and began training local girls in illumination. He supplied them with copies of Modern Art magazine and had them water color the decorative initials used in the articles.

As demand for the books grew and the subscription list of The Philistine expanded, more equipment was added and more space was needed. Construction began in November 1898 to enlarge the printing shop and in early 1899 ground was broken for the Phalanstery. This building would eventually absorb the first printing shop. By August of 1899 another building was taking shape across South Grove Street at the comer of Main Street. There is an interesting sidelight here that illustrates Elbert Hubbard's skill as an entrepreneur. He advertised that he would pay one dollar a wagon load for field stone delivered to his new building site. The local farmers began delivering load after load of stone to the "fool" who would pay good money for the stone that littered their fields. If the farmer's had stopped to consider the time and labor involved in picking up, delivering and unloading at Hubbard's building site one full wagon load of field stone they might have wondered who really was the fool!

The loads of stone delivered became the Chapel and was as the name implies, to house the typesetting functions. However, the typesetting area was never transferred there and the building was used as the offices, gift shop and bank. It now houses the offices of the Town of Aurora in which East Aurora is a village.

An L-shaped building in back of the Chapel was also constructed from the field stone and housed the printing, typesetting, bindery and shipping functions. The bindery was later moved to the furniture shop building when that function was discontinued. Exactly what equipment was added in 1899 is still unknown but the East Aurora Advertiser of December 1, 1899 mentioned that forty-seven Roycrofters had a turkey dinner on that date and Dirlam/Simmons mentions sixty employees in the same year. Whatever the true number we can still see a tremendous increase in the work force since the inception of the shops.

The bindery was the next major addition after the move of the printing and typesetting equipment.

The first books produced had been sent into Buffalo for binding while The Philistine was hand folded and stitched at the Roycroft shop with the two stitchers acquired from the Pendennis Press.

There was no direct supervision in the bindery and with the increase in magazine press runs and inquiries from early subscribers on binding their Philistines into annuals it became time to look for a binder.

In 1896 Hubbard announced that a master binder "direct from Liepsic" would organize the Roycroft bindery. The master binder was the Louis H. Kinder mentioned earlier. Hubbard was right in describing Kinder as a master binder but he was not "direct from Liepsic". Kinder was working in Buffalo when he agreed to move to East Aurora. He was born in Germany and was a third generation bookbinder as well as a most accomplished paper marbler. He had published an American edition of Josef Halfer's *Progress of the Marbling Art, From Technical Scientific Principles, With a Supplement on the Decoration of Book Edges* in 1894. The announcement in The American Bookmaker of February 1894 that this book would be the subscription premium and describing the work as copyrighted by Louis H. Kinder of Buffalo, New York places Kinder in Buffalo and not in Hubbard's "Liepsic".

Kinder quickly established the bindery on the second floor of the new building behind the Chapel and assumed supervision and training of the local workers. He organized production in the mechanical side of the bindery and began to assemble the equipment for the hand bindery. The photographs show some of the bindery areas. The magazines were machine folded and stitched and in the peak years of production employed about fifty girls. The regular editions of the books were sewn on the Smythe machine while the books for special treatment in illumination and/or binding were hand sewn on the frames. By 1913 the bindery had six folding machines with Cross automatic feeders and there were three Smythe sewing machines. There were sufficient wire stitchers and bundlers to handle the large monthly runs of The Philistine, Little Journeys and Fra plus the assorted advertising booklets published.

The hand bindery had its own Smythe machine for sewing those editions that had special binding treatment but were not limited editions. Three stamping presses plus the leather forming equipment were in the hand binding area.

With the bindery set up on the second floor of the new building, printing equipment and type facilities could be expanded on the ground floor and basement. Only ads and some personal reminiscences document the years preceding 1912, the year of publication of Chandler's article.[46]

An ad for Colt Armory presses in The American Printer in 1901 boasts that six Half-Super Royal Colts were in use at the Roycroft shop. There is evidence[47] of major equipment purchases in 1907. On February 7th a Harris two color rotary was installed. On April 1st an auto-feeder was ordered for the new Babcock cylinder press and the 40" x 50" Optimus press was installed on April 25th. In June the electric generation station was installed on the Roycroft campus to insure sufficient power for all of the shops.

Another ad of the same era stated that a Whitlock press had been used almost exclusively for all of the large press runs at Roycroft since the shop's inception. Since Elbert Hubbard wrote the ad, we can doubt the extent of use but not the existence of the Whitlock.

Lyman Chandler's article best describes the physical plant in 1912. The shop then had twelve Colt Armory presses for the book work. The Philistine and other large run periodicals were run on the 62" Huber and Hodgson, the Babcock or the four 56" cylinder or three 38" cylinder pony presses. There was the two color Harris mentioned earlier and two presses used for printing the photogravures. All of the presses were equipped with Cross automatic feeders and there were two large power paper cutters.

The photogravures were produced in the tower. Those used in the early books were furnished by the Color Company of New York City. Establishing a photogravure processing section within the Roycroft plant was encouraged by Cy Rosen to insure an adequate supply of plates. A photogravure and plate making shop were installed in the bindery tower in 1907 to solve production problems caused by waitting for the delivery of plates from New York.

The shop moved quickly away from the inferior papers used in the first two books. Paper in the Roycroft books is generally of high quality; Boxmoor being an unfortunate choice. An article in the local newspaper of November 7, 1907 tells us that the shop purchased most of its machine made and handmade papers, excluding Fabriano, from Perkins, Goodwin & Co. This same information was later repeated as an ad in the Fra for the paper merchants.

The Fabriano papers had the Roycroft watermark and were purchased directly from the mill. According to the same article the shop purchased $10,000 worth of paper from Fabriano alone that year.

The type used in the shop was either foundry cast or Monotype. The foundry type was purchased from American Type Founders or Keystone Type Foundry while the shop purchased Monotype sorts from the Empire Type Foundry of Delevan, New York until it acquired its first Monotype machinery in 1903. (Later expanded in 1908.) The Monotype units were used to set The Philistine and the Fra as composition matter and to cast the sorts to keep the cases filled for the hand setting of the books. New foundry type faces were frequently purchased and the books show an excellent use of the contemporary type faces. The Roycroft shop was among the first to use Cheltenham and Kennerly and to use them well.

Although the shop never commissioned a type face it did use the available faces very wisely. The typography of the books shows a professional level understanding of a type face and its relationship to the page. The new type faces were not used in the common material but were introduced in the special titles handled by the Roycroft staff designers and typographers.

The Roycroft shop has been criticized for not following the direction of the English presses in having its own "look". I personally find the work of the Roycroft shops to be much more visually exciting than the work of these presses. Granted that there is an overall greater production quality in the books of the English presses the broad range of experimentation found in the Roycroft books is much more interesting to the modern graphic designer.

THE PRODUCTS

William Marian Reedy,that astute observerof Elbert Hubbard ,remarked: "It has been said, by myself and others, that Hubbard's appeal is to the half-baked. Culture is relative. People who follow Hubbard do not stay half-baked. They come out of it; he makes lovers of books out of people who never knew books before."[48]

Perhaps he did bring people to fine books but his own goal was to promote himself through a salable product. Elbert Hubbard was not the American disciple of William Morris nor did he intentionally promote American graphic design; he was a writer of very mediocre literary material who was a genius at promotion.

Hubbard has to be considered the originator of much of modern advertising techniques. He perfected the unsolicited delivery of merchandise and the free trial. He knew that what worked for soap would work for books. He used endorsements, solicited and unsolicited, from the well-known to advertise his books. He knew his audience and he wrote to them. He knew that appearance was becoming more important in selling than quality or durability.

Hubbard built the Roycroft enterprise on two premises learned in his soap-peddling days. One was that people were basically honest and would pay for what they used or kept. Secondly, there were others who would find him and his philosophy personally appealing. They were the unsettled, the creatively unsatisfied, who wanted some outlet for their supposed talents or at least somewhere to place their enthusiasm. The clerks, office managers, supervisors and self-employed small businessmen were his audience. They were the "Belle Epoque" in shirt protectors. They might quote Oscar Wilde but never defend him; they wanted their literary excitement plainly packaged. Hubbard gave them his own version of Taber's The Philistine.

The Philistine

The most successful products of the Roycroft Printing Shop were the little magazines: The Philistine, Fra, Little Journeys, and Roycroft Quarterlies introduced Hubbard and sold the books while selling

Hubbard wrote. It was following the lead of other small magazines used to promote hard cover editions produced the the press.

The Philistine was supposed to be the journal of the Society of The Philistines. Membership in the society brought one year of the monthly for free while non-members paid one dollar for the subscription. The society had one meeting, the infamous Stephen Crane affair, but the magazine lasted twenty years.

The Philistine belongs to the little magazine or "Purple Cow" period. Faxon's bibliography[49] lists 241 serials produced from 1893 to 1903. They were mostly periodicals of protest or satire and often rather crude in their content as well as in their physical appearance. They called themselves the Alkahest, Bauble, Gauntlet, Honey Jar, Impressions, Jester, Knocker, etc. and so on through the alphabet. Some lasted one issue, some one year and a few are counted in years rather than issues.

The little magazines reflected their originators, and The Philistine shares this trait with its more worthy contemporaries. When Harry Taber started it in 1895 there was no prediction of a future. The first issue was printed in a press run of 2500 copies. It was sent free to the "literati", a few were sold at ten cents per copy and fewer still subscriptions at $1.00 per year subscriptions were received. It contained an article on ancient and modern Philistines by William McIntosh, the editor of the Buffalo Evening News, an article on English monuments by Elbert Hubbard and the SideTalks section by Taber. This section was to be the fun part. This issue had a spoof of the "Side Talks with Girls" written by Edward Bok of the Ladies Home Journal under the pen name of Ruth Ashmore. Bliss Carmen was scolded for plagiarism, and Mark Twain was told not to worry about people taking his Joan of Arc as humor since it had been a long time since he had written any good humor. William Dean Howells and Stephen Crane were lampooned. This first Side Talks finished with a critique of the magazines of the day. Scribner's "has a thrilling article on 'Books We Have Published'" while The Century, it said, will insert a page or two of reading matter between the Italian Art and the ads." There were some poems and digs at The Chapbook which became The Chipmunk Thomas Mosher was mildly insulted and one can suppose that a good time was had by all in putting this first issue together. Side Talks had that feeling of turn of the century collegiate humor that was juvenile and did no harm.

When Elbert Hubbard took over in the February 1896 issue there was no immediate change in the substance of the magazine. Succeeding issues carried the work of William Blackburn Harte, William Morris, Rudyard Kipling, Gelett Burgess, Carolyn Wells, Joaquin Miller, Ouida and Yone Noguchi. The jabs continued at their favorite targets, William Dean Howells and Edward Bok. Stone and Kimball became Rock and Bumble and Mosher's Bibelot and other little magazines were gently roasted. The first year's issues of the magazine are quite readable.

The mood of the magazine changed when Hubbard turned it to his own taste. By the March 1897 issue there were no longer any literary pretensions. The contributors were all unknowns except Stephen Crane and more of the magazine was given over to advertising. Surprisingly, in this area of promotion Elbert Hubbard met his match.

Hubbard had sold the right to market the advertising space in The Philistine to one Fred Gardner of Chicago. Gardner was to sell the advertising space and pay Hubbard a flat monthly commission. Felix Shay[50] mentions the sum of five hundred dollars a month and that the contract was to run for ninety-nine years. Five hundred a month has to be wrong. No advertising agent would pay that great sum of nineteenth century dollars for the rights to a potential nothing. Whatever the true amount it was still not important since there were very few advertisers in the first issues and they were low paying literary inserts. However, as the magazine grew in popularity more and better paying ads were placed and Hubbard saw the agreement turn against him. Now Gardner was selling the space at his own rate and forwarding Hubbard a flat payment. Hubbard tried to first cancel the contract and when Gardner refused he started to sell space in violation of the contract. Gardner sued several times for payment of all revenues collected by Hubbard and finally Hubbard gave up and bought Gardner out. Clarence P. O'Dell was appointed circulation manager for the magazine in 1902 and Hubbard took control of the advertising revenues.

Advertising had started in the second issue with the front foldover cover being taken by Thomas Bird Mosher for his Bibelot. Other space was taken by an antiquarian bookseller, the Pendennis Press, Putnam's to promote the Little Journeys and the back cover advertised a book by Walter Blackburn Harte. Tracing the advertising growth and its direction clearly demonstrates the transition from literary emphasis to pure mercantilism. The early issues carried advertising for the other little magazines and current hard cover publications from the small avantgarde publishers such as Way and Williams. Ads placed in The Philistine by these advertisers added a legitimacy to the new magazine. The change in advertisers from the May 1897 issue tells us how the magazine was changing. Now there are three ads for bicycles and two for sanitariums. The Bibelot ad disappears from the inside front cover and one for the Roycroft's *In the Track of the Bookworm* took its place. Mosher' s ad was the last any quality publisher would take in The Philistine.

In the June 1897 issue ads for a breakfast food and a thermal bath joined the bicycles and sanitariums. In July another cereal is added to the advertising list. The September 1897 issue contained the first sneak ad for a client. This was an advertising trick that Elbert Hubbard must have invented or surely perfected. The first essay in this number related the efforts of the massage boy at the Jackson Sanitarium of Dansville, New York. Coincidentally, the back page of the issue has an ad for the place.

Railroads signed up along with the typewriter makers for the next issue. They were soon joined by ads for metaphysical magazines and patent medicines. To accommodate the demand for advertising space the magazine had started with quarter page ads in the December 1898 issue. Half-tone cuts soon appeared and the magazine was divided into two sections. The front was printed on the regular book stock while advertisements were relegated to the back and printed on cheap stock.

Ads for automobiles, art studios, cures, refrigerators, etc. surrounded the shrinking literary content until by June 1901 the average issue consisted of sixteen pages of frontispiece advertising, thirty-two pages of copy and sixteen pages more of advertising. Considering that the thirty-two pages of "literary" content were usually a self-promotion of Elbert Hubbard, the Philistine could no longer be considered to have any literary merit. If any lingering hope remained with those who had encouraged the little magazine those hopes were destroyed with the manifesto that appeared in the January 1899 issue.

A MANIFESTO

Beginning with the next number of this magazine, I propose to write every article and paragraph in it, including advertisements and testimonials of Roycroft books. If it were possible to secure anyone to write so well as myself I would not do this. But compare the signed articles in any PHILISTINE with my Heart to Heart Talks and see if you can blame me for the decision I have come to or the decision to which I have come. To be sure, these articles are better than anything to be found in Harpies or the Eighteenth Century, yet they still lack fosforus and must be rated in Class B. Literature should contain ginger, also besom, for these make up that undeniable something which stamps the work as Classic Art. And the PHILISTINE must be of such quality that a hundred years from now every number will be worth as many dollars. This cannot be the case if I continue to immortalize the machine-made goods of Marco Morrow and Michael Monahan. They form too heavy a tail to the kite.

Then note the iniquities of Stephen Crane and the deeply dekel-edge filosofy of William McIntosh and marvel at the miracle of succeeding in spite of the handicap!

All of these men named, I have fed, clothed and lodged for two years. To be sure, as Chester Lord tauntingly avers, they have slept three to a bed, but I have fed them well, and given them every encouragement to persevere in an artistic career and make men of themselves. I suppose no publisher in America has been so harried by the ubiquitous socio-literary Cave-of-the-Winds, as I. One of my legs is now so much longer than the other that I can only walk by the aid of a crutch. But these batty poets, who soar high and dive deep, and never pay cash, have pusht the game just a little too far. I am done with the whole regiment of Ruf Writers; and all parties are notified not to hitch their wagons to this Star. In an attempt to work out a Theory in Social Science I started a Book Farm and took in sundry brace of hungry archangels (a little battered), treating them as brothers. Behold the result!

Starting with Harry Taber, to whom I paid four dollars a week and board, my cubbard (also my buffet) has been made desolate. Through the exploitation of these greedly literary varlets, who sang the Song of Vagabondia at my expense to a rag and a bone and a hank of hair, I am not able to give my poor dog a bone. One day in February, 1896 I went away on a lecturing tour, leaving Harry Taber in charge. I was gone just three days, and when I came back I found Master Harry had organized a stock company, with seventeen others of his ilk, including a pudgy poet known to the police as Dick White, and this merry group had actually started another magazine with intent to either Bust the PHILISTINE or make me sell out cheap.

I gave Harry Taber just one kick in the pants, and continued serenely on my way.

Next Walter Blackburn Harte came down upon me, and he was the finest o' the lot. He remained in East Aurora two weeks (lacking one day) and didn't do a thing while he was here but tie fire-crackers to my coat-tail. He then towsled his hair like a boofay artist, curst in falsetto, and rusht into "Footlights" and another sheet like it, called "The Critic," telling why East Aurora was no place for a man of genius, and declaring I was a big What-D'ye-Call-It......

Blackhart further instigated the Associated Press to send out a dispatch stating I had been drowned in the Irish Sea and that as I had the Society of the Philistines in my vest pocket, the American Academy of Immortals was No More.

Jeanette Gilder, of the Gilder Family-Robinson, took sides against me because I had firmly refused to publish her stuff-(there being too much Ego in her cosmos): and hell hath no fury like a woman-author scorned. Jeanette ventilated in her fashion journal the exacerbation's of the Blackhart Fice, and besides repeating all of his libels declared over her own signature that I was an octopus.

About the time Blackhart was running the "Lotus" on the reef, Irving Browne thought he would go out to East Aurora and look at the hole in the ground where the PHILISTINE once was, and strew a few cockle-burrs 'er my grave. He found me alive and kicking.

He also saw Michael Monahan hard at work smoking, under my own vine and fig tree, and in surprise exclaimed, "Why I thought you were drowned by the Irish-See?"

After Blackhart had gone back to Bloomingdale, there arrived three rogues in buckram, by name: John Jerome Rooney, Steve Crane and Ramlin Whidden. None of them could write much better than Philip Becker Goetz, but all had ambitions, and a Thirst.

Strict East Aurora asceticism was not to Stevie's taste. He went down to New York in search of Local Color and evidently found it, for he came back daubed all over-his karacter specked as a turkey's egg.

Stevie's next move was to pinch eight thousand dollars that Amy Leslie had entrusted him to carry to the bank. It was Amy's whole month's salary as editor of the "Chicago News" Society Page. Stevie did not get away with the boodle, however, for Amy went after him, caught him, took the money out of the front of his calico waist where he had stuft it, and cautioned him never to do so again. After that I positively refused to have anything to do with Steve: had he secured the eight thousand (or Amy) it might have been different.

Marco Morrow and Bliss Carmen then came to take Steve's place. Neither one proved facile or felicitous in handling a pitch-fork, and Ignorance (which is Bliss) was so bright that he would not get up mornings until noon, as he said he wished to give the Dawn a chance.

I do not care to speak ill of anyone, but truth compels me to say that Richard Hovey, whom I carried thru two hard winters, showed his total unfitness for communal life by refusing to churn, and Tudor Jenks wrote no poetry after the cider barrel was empty. So I turn 'em both out.

I have recently had applications to join my Colony from Stanley Waterloo, DeWitt Miller, Hawley Smith, Ernest H. Crosby, Hayden Carruth, Yone Noguchi, Jos. Leon Gobeille, and James Jeffrey Roche (who signs himself "Late of County Down"), but to each and all my reply has been the same: Go rub your head against the vest front of B. O. Flowers.

And so from working for the good of all, I intend hereafter to practice Individualism, and write the whole Magazine myself, just for my own amusement.

All those proposing to cancel subscriptions must pay up dues to date.
                                                                    -The Pastor.

The "Manifesto" can be taken as a tongue-in-cheek harangue or as a real attack upon those who Hubbard would discredit as associates of the magazine. Whatever, it is a clever statement. He excoriates Taber and Harte and turns to gentle spoofing to dismiss the rest.

After the manifesto any contributions to The Philistine not written by Hubbard were promotions for a Roycroft book or for an advertiser. Essays became "preachments" from The Pastor to his flock and that flock did multiply.

The Philistine lasted twenty years and one month. Circulation figures reveal the public's acceptance of the magazine (and of Elbert Hubbard). The circulation went from 2,500 copies printed in 1895 to 52,000 copies sold in 1898. The circulation figure went up to 90,000 and finally topped off at 102,000 in 1902. Champney credits it with 110,000 and that is a rather amazing figure when one considers that Stone and Kimball's Chapbook, a really superior publication, never exceeded a circulation of 16,500. Of course, each had its own audience.

The circulation figures given above were taken from The Philistine and may be considered accurate. The one ledger of the Roycroft shop that has survived is for 1909/10 and gives us these figures. It shows 445 new subscriptions and 214 renewals for the month of August 1909. Taken as average those are healthy figures considering the magazine had peaked in 1901/02.

In contrast to its betters the magazine must have survived only because of Elbert Hubbard. It never would have survived on its physical attractiveness.

The printing quality ranged from good to bad and generally ranged closer to the bad. Although its physical appearance varied during its first few years, it settled down to a standard format of mustard color rough stock for the cover, kraft paper for the ads and natural color laid paper for the essay material.

The progression to this format started with the first issue in one color on natural laid stock with a one ply cover. The second issue shows a lighter weight cover stock in two colors, red and black, with refined typography and the full front cover fold-over that carried the Bibelot ad. The butcher cover paper finally adopted appeared in the fourth issue with the fold-over gone and the cheap kraft paper carrying the ads front and back. This format changes to a red paper cover for the Christmas issue of 1895, then reverts back to butcher paper. The color of the cover stock changes from mustard to light gray in the May 1896 issue, and the fold-over returns in June 1896. This continues to February 1897 with the Christmas issue done in a pink paper cover. February 1897 shows a brown-gray cover that continues until June 1897. The July and August issues revert to light gray and then back to the brown-gray until the mustard stock returns in February 1898.

Mustard remained the standard cover stock until the publication ceased. The interior stock varied at times for the same reason that the cover stock varied-availability and price.

In summation, the best of The Philistines in both editorial and graphic content were the earliest. In its later years, the graphic quality of the magazine matched the editorial content-very weak.

There was one failing of The Philistine that could not be overcome. Since it was a Little Magazine it had to stay little and advertisers found the size too limiting and too expensive for the format offered. Not only would the advertiser get less space, they could not use existing plates and hence incurred additional make-ready expenses. The Roycroft shop answered with The Fra.

The Fra

The Fra was started in 1908 to accommodate those national advertisers who could not economically use The Philistine. It was a large magazine, 9" x14" and could not only fit the plates used in the national magazines but was printed on coated stock to insure good half-tone reproduction; another fault of The Philistine.

It was certainly more attractive than The Philistine since it was designed by Dard Hunter. In content it also had more to say on current issues since Alice wrote the best material for the magazine and encouraged new contributors. Elbert's contributions were reprints of Philistine pieces and the copy for the ads. It sold for 25 cents a month or two dollars per year and the ledger noted earlier tells us that there were 811 new and 253 renewals for August 1909. It was a good source of revenue for the Hubbards since the ads that Hubbard wrote were always captioned "An Advertisement by Elbert Hubbard", telling us that Hubbard was becoming more ad writer than essayist at that point in his career. The Fra lasted until September 1917 when it was replaced by The Roycroft Magazine.

The Roycroft Magazine
This was a return to the butcher paper covered format though larger than The Philistine. It had nothing of interest to offer and was replaced by The Roycrofter which also showed the total lack of inventiveness of the enterprise after the death of the Hubbards in 1915.

The Roycroft Quarterlies
Another series which lost Elbert Hubbard's interest earlier in the history of the shop was The Roycroft Quarterly. Three issues were published and then it stopped. It was interesting because it was unlike the other early Roycroft publications in flavor and makeup. It also shows what might have been. The first issue featured Stephen Crane and was issued in May 1896. The second, published in August 1896 marked the first appearance in separate form of George Bernard Shaw's On Going to Church and the third was Foreign Ideas in the Catholic Church by Father George Zurcher. The publication of this third Quarterly in November 1896 finished the series.

In format the Quarterlies differed markedly from The Philistine and Little Journeys. In fact, the three issues were all different formats. The first two Quarterlies measured roughly 7" x 5" while the third was larger at 9" x 6". They were well printed and the literary content was certainly higher than average for a Roycroft title. The Crane number content had already appeared in The Philistine, and it was the editing done by Hubbard for the second Quarterly that brought Shaw's justifiable wrath upon Hubbard. The third, the Father Zurcher essay, was controversial for its time and Hubbard showed courage in publishing it.

There are a number of points in the series designs worth noting. The Crane number used a variation of the cover design for the Philistine Society dinner for Crane while the Shaw number used a Kelmscott style border in red on coarse brown paper. The Zurcher is the most interesting bibliographically. Its large format suggests that the piece was not printed at the Roycroft shop. There was no reason to change the size and format and the text type is Caslon, which was not in the shop's cases in 1896. The paper stock is a machine made laid variety seen only in this one publication. The composition is quite commercial and what one would expect from a commercial printer of the time. I suspect that the pamphlet was printed by Father Zurcher and offered to or solicited by Elbert Hubbard for distribution with the Roycroft imprint. Nevertheless, they all expired before building a following for the series. Another series was started that was evidently more to Hubbard's taste and to that of his audience; The Little Journeys.

The Little Journeys
The Little Journeys were Elbert Hubbard and Alice Moore's first venture. She provided the encouragement when they were seeing each other in Boston. Harry Taber's involvement has been related earlier as well as Putnam's acceptance of the idea. They offered Hubbard thirty dollars an essay to be delivered monthly.

The Journeys were neither biographical nor historical, and however badly written and researched they were successful. Hubbard took over publication from Putnam's in 1900. Although the details of the transfer are unknown it is evident that part of the agreement was Hubbard's permission for Putnam's to continue to publish those titles already issued by them and that Hubbard would not duplicate those Little Journeys. Putnam's could not have been pleased to have this series pass out of its hands since every journey had gone beyond ten printings in the bound volumes and the most popular, *Little Journeys to the Homes of Famous Women*, went to twenty thousand copies.

The formats of the two series of Little Journeys were quite different. The Putnam's series was rather in the style of the Chapbooks, 7" x 5¾", printed in two colors and issued in a conservative typographical format. The Roycroft Little Journeys gave the shop its ill-deserved reputation as copyists of the Kelmscott Press. They had heavy borders and an overprinting caused by printing the heavy hand made paper dry. They in fact shared many of the faults of that English press. The Little Journeys were really Roycroft's only aping of Kelmscott and I feel that they were not better looking because the format was acceptable to the audience and the graphic artists at the shop had more interesting work to do. Later, changes were made in the design and the series culminated with the Dard Hunter Little Journeys to the Homes of Great Businessmen.

Whatever their physical appearance they sold well. They were issued monthly in paper at 25 cents per copy and offered in two volume annuals at $3.00 for suede binding or $5.00 for three quarter leather. A deluxe edition was also offered monthly and annually. This deluxe edition was hand illumined, which was really hand coloring of the initial letters and borders. The deluxe edition sold for $1.00 per issue, $12.00 for the annuals.

The monthly issues were paginated serially, and those sold by subscription or sent to life members were bound. The sheets not bound were stored for the annual or for special orders. Special illumination ceased with Eminent Orators in 1903. The design did not change then but we must assume that the illumination studio found the demand too heavy and the shop (Hubbard) could get a better return on the illuminator's time than the one dollar per issue for Little Journeys.

The subscription figures available show 32,000 subscribers in 1909/10 and this figure may be in the decline of the popularity of the series. Putnam's series, the earliest group, covered Good Men and Great, Authors, Famous Women, American Statesmen and Eminent Painters. These subject headings left little for Hubbard to work with. He did some duplication and reworked some of Putnam's material but sales were hindered by the duplication. Incidentally, there is one duplication in the Hubbard series. The William Morris Little Journey was done twice but the two editions are quite different in format and cannot be confused.

The sales structure of the Little Journeys is another example of Elbert Hubbard's merchandising ability. Buyers would order one copy of the single issue and then be persuaded by mail solicitation to order another deluxe copy for a friend or as an investment. The same customers would then often order the bound annual. The Roycroft shop did have loyal customers but we have seen correspondence that shows that Hubbard could go wrong.

Subscribers to the Little Journey could return copies to be bound into three quarter suede volumes for a $1.50 binding charge per pamphlet.

Bert Hubbard wondered about this practice as per this exchange of correspondence.[51]

Bert Hubbard to Alice Hubbard, August 24, 1910.
I notice that when our customers ask permission to return paper bound copies of the Little Journeys in pamphlet form and receive credit for them they are not allowed to do so and when they want pamphlet copies bound up they are obliged to return their own copies and have them individually bound for which we charge them $1.50. This is board binding and has the paper label on the back. The regular $2.00 copies of Little

Journeys are on hand made paper and have a leather label on the back. These are bound up in quantities. It seems to me that it is very poor policy on our part to insist on having the pamphlet copies returned and binding them individually when we might just as well allow five cents a copy for the pamphlets and send the regular $2.00 from stock avoiding the unnecessary work of handling individual binding orders. Inquiring regarding this of our correspondents I was advised that they had been instructed by you to carry out binding orders for Little Journeys in the way that it is being done now.

In my opinion this scheme should be changed as I have suggested and I submit it to you.

(signed)

(Alice's reply on August 25)

The matter of the Little Journeys that you bring to my attention is one that Mr. Hubbard brought to my attention about two years ago with the emphatic remark that "we are selling Little Journeys not buying them" and to have no more bought. I believe that you will see that this is in the line of business.

I corrected this in the office as soon as your father asked me to do so. However, this is a self limiting proposition as there are no new Little Journeys coming out and the end is in sight . Thank you for calling my attention to it and I remain. (signed)

By 1910 Hubbard saw that public interest in his Little Journeys was waning and that prospects in the other Roycroft publications for possible new series and for soliciting themes was drawing little response. He turned to a new audience for his talents. Big business. The last essays written as Little Journeys were the Little Journeys to the Homes of Great Businessmen. Hubbard found that he was quite comfortable in their homes and they appreciated his selling talents. As the orders for individual essays from the series poured in from the companies and/or associates of the essay subjects he must have seen a great new potential.

The first example of Hubbard's skill as a propagandist was the material inserted in the early Philistines as editorial material that was really an advertisement. Now he used the Little Journeys the same way. Except for using the editorial material as a lead-in, it became the selling tool as a Little Journey. He started by writing the essay and presenting it to the subject of the essay. The first response was from Mr. James Oliver of the Oliver Chilled Plow Works. After the publication of Mr. Oliver's life as a regular Little Journey another press run was purchased by the plow company. Other Journeys were purchased by Jac Auer, a health studio operator, John Jacob Astor, John B. Stetson, Andrew Taylor Still and John D. Rockefeller. These commercial Little Journeys degenerated into blurbs in pamphlet form for anyone with the price. The Journeys noted above were done with some taste in production; later Journeys were just produced for the profit.

Public response to the Little Journeys may be measured by the same ledger noted earlier. While this ledger carried 445 new and 214 renewals for The Philistine in 1909/10 there were only 3 new and no renewals recorded for the Little Journeys. It was clear that they had lost their popularity and would no longer be a source of revenue for the shop and for Elbert Hubbard.

If the Little Journeys were done as money makers let us look at the one publication that was always profitable for Elbert Hubbard both in money and popularity.-The Message to Garcia.

The Message to Garcia
What would have happened to Elbert Hubbard and the Roycroft shop if he had not written the Message to Garcia? The timing of the piece probably was less important than its appearance. It thrust Hubbard into the mainstream of American political and social thought. His audience and client list mushroomed because of this one short essay. The content of the message and its implications are beyond our scope, but the printing history is important to us.

The essay first appeared in the March 1899 issue of The Philistine as a short untitled piece. Bert Hubbard tells us in his Impressions[52] that he and his father were discussing Rowan's adventure and Hubbard felt that the Cuban general was the hero. Bert disagreed saying it was Rowan since he had traveled through hostile country while the Cuban could just have easily traveled to meet him. Hubbard, in his own account of the incident saw that the boy was right, went to his desk and wrote the essay in one sitting. This was in February; the next month he included the piece in his Talks.

Within days of the issue's distribution orders for extra copies for that number of the Phil started coming in to the shop. The demand continued at a moderate rate until George H. Daniels, General Passenger Agent for the New York Central Railroad, cabled Hubbard asking for a price quote and earliest shipping date for 100,000 copies with a New York Central advertisement on the back cover. Hubbard supposedly replied that he only had three foot-operated presses[53] and estimated that it would take the shop two years of constant work to complete that order. He therefore gave Mr. Daniels permission to have the essay reprinted by a commercial printer.

In 1902, Daniels told a meeting of the New York City Universalist Club[54] that he had printed and distributed one million copies of the message in the three years since Hubbard had written it. The Roycroft shop did print four early editions of the essay and these are the first series of many editions of the work done at the shop. The first Roycroft printing was an edition of 1,000 copies, and the three subsequent editions were of 920, 928 and 925 copies. All four share the same format; only the limiting statement was changed. The first edition of these first printings can be distinguished by the subtitle, Being a Small Homily by Elbert Hubbard. All subsequent editions are subtitled Being a Preachment by Elbert Hubbard.

Daniels had also issued the Message as one of The Four Track Series, the company magazine. He put this notice on the title page: "Having received so many requests from clergymen, teachers and others interested in educational work, we have decided, with the kind permission of the author, to make A Message to Garcia one of the Four Track Series and to print it in editions of 100,000 until the demand is satisfied, if it takes the entire 20th century to accomplish it."

The Roycrofters also continued to issue editions of the Message. It became the bread and butter item so dearly loved by commercial printers and sometimes referred to as "printing the mortgage". It did that for the Roycrofters! They printed it in every conceivable format. There were small paper bound, large paper bound and the usual limited editions. Hubbard did one very interesting limited edition. This is the limited edition signed by Hubbard and Rowan. A letter from Rowan to Lyman Chandler dated September 17,1903 asks for specific instructions on signing the one hundred sheets sent for his signature.[55] Apparently the signature of both men on the flyleaf was supposed to signify some association. Though Rowan had visited Roycroft in July of that year he signed the sheets in Atchison, Kansas.

In 1901 the Roycrofters offered A Message to Garcia and Thirteen Other Things. It was available in the regular edition bound in boards, and as an edition of fifty copies done on Japan Vellum, hand illumined and bound in full levant and "a few copies with pages of the original manuscript bound in." Actually Elbert Hubbard had given the manuscript for the Message to the Grosvenor library[56] in 1900. It is still there and is quite complete. Hubbard and company used photogravured facsimiles. The Message to Garcia gave Hubbard recognition and revenue and he used the first to increase the second.

The message that Hubbard himself got from the Message to Garcia and the Little Journeys written for businessmen was that advertising paid and he had a way to get well paid. He started offering advertising booklets written to order. Over four hundred have been cataloged to date. Not all were written by Hubbard, but the "messages" would be written in Hubbard's style and touched up by the Fra himself. These are small booklets, usually around 4" x 6" and twenty pages in length. Most are uninteresting designs, the exceptions being those done by Dard Hunter. Hunter also designed some advertising material for the other shops as well. Motto sheets and cards carrying the epigrams of Elbert Hubbard were sold through the inn, gift shop and in the book catalogs. Hunter designed many of these sheets as well as a calendar and a portfolio of the Roycroft campus (1910). The design staff created bookplates to order for $25.00 to $35.00 each and many of these are quite interesting designs. The posters done by Collins and Denslow as well as the enlarged cartoons by Denslow are also important ephemera in the history of the printing shop. All of the ephemeral material, magazines and catalogs were created for one purpose-to sell books and Elbert Hubbard.

It is the selling of the books that shows us the advertising genius of Elbert Hubbard.

The Books

Hubbard attracted his audience through The Philistine, kept them with its content and used that publication and the others described above to move the books. The books were made "arty" for their audience and were the "culture" referred to by Reedy. The standard binding was suede because that was the trendy binding material of the time. The Roycroft Shop bindery did not originate this horrible binding; they copied the commercial publishers of the day.

The titles issued by the press tell us the tastes of the audience. *The Songs of Songs* and *Journal of Koheleth* were Taber titles and sold badly. Even when Hubbard had established his following neither title was reprinted though Hubbard was closely associated with both. *Art and Life, Ruskin-Turner* and *Glynne's Wife* were more to the liking of the modern literati at the turn of the last century. Shaw's *On Going To Church* and Hubbard's *The Legacy* were apparently accepted by the followers of the press as serious literature. The books published by the press can be divided into four categories: first, the writings of Elbert Hubbard; second known contemporary authors whose work he printed with or without permission; third, the copyright free classics that were the mainstay of the private presses, and last were the unknowns who paid Hubbard to print and distribute their work without royalty. This last group provided Hubbard income and the authors with an outlet other than the known vanity presses or self-publication. Julia Ditto Young, Adeline Knapp, Lucian Foote among others were published by the Roycroft Shop under contracts favorable only to Elbert Hubbard.

Mrs. Young paid Hubbard $325 for *Glynne's Wife* in a contract dated May 11, 1896.[57] The book was to be printed and distributed by the Roycroft Shop. She also contracted for the shop to do her The Story of Saville for $275. This contract[58] called for two color printing but excluded binding (which would be done in Buffalo anyway). Hubbard was to advertise and sell the book for a twenty percent commission. There is no evidence of the contractual arrangement made with William Marion Reedy or others who had some following but the terms were probably more equitable.

The classics were among the best designed books offered by the press. They were well-printed and bound and were probably of no personal interest to Elbert Hubbard.

The printing of well-known authors is the category that condemns Hubbard. He printed Crane, Kipling and Shaw and bastardized each one's work. Hubbard laughed off the criticism. Here again is that flaw in Hubbard. He published work that none but a vanity publisher would touch and also published work that deserved exposure but twisted that work; degraded it with his own ego satisfaction. Publishing the work of Stephen Crane, Rudyard Kipling and George Bernard Shaw could have given Hubbard a greater role in American letters than Thomas Mosher. Where Mosher's books are delicate and not very exciting visually, the Roycroft material has an exuberance that lends much to the total work. As Reedy remarked, Hubbard had an audience that he really could have educated. Instead he gave them Hubbard.

The writings of Elbert Hubbard were the press' best sellers. Multiple printings of *Time and Chance, The Man of Sorrow* and Health and Wealth attested to his popularity.

The literary quality of Hubbard's work is not within the scope of this text but there is one point that is worth noting. Most of the work of

Elbert Hubbard published by the Roycroft is quite mediocre in design. I find this interesting. Why would the books done by the proprietor of the enterprise be the least attractive? The William Morris title is really the only non-Dard Hunter title that is attractive. The books designed by Dard Hunter are interesting but even Hunter's work on the Alice Moore Hubbard titles is far superior. Perhaps Hubbard felt that expending extra effort in designing, printing or illuminating his titles would be a waste of effort and money. He was probably right. They would sell anyway and the designers and production skills could be reserved for those titles that would have to sell on their appearance. It is a valid point.

Another point of considerable interest is the markedly higher quality of the graphic design of Alice Hubbard's titles. Her own works as well as her joint efforts with Elbert were designed by Dard Hunter. We know that Hunter liked Alice and probably enjoyed working with her but there is evidence that she may have been the promoter of the better book designs done during her tenure in the shop. One of the best designed books issued is her Garnett and the Brindled Cow which was done after Hunter had left the shop. I do wish some solid evidence of her position on the design of books has been found during this investigation. I have a feeling that she had to have had as strong an influence on this aspect of the shop operation as we know she had in other parts.

Whatever the books looked like they had to be sold and again Elbert Hubbard proved to be a master of the art of promotion.

The first promotional scheme used for the books was one that had worked for the Larkin soap products. Like the soap products the books were offered on free trial use. New issues of the press were sent to Philistine subscribers and book collectors known to Hubbard "on suspicion" as it was termed.

The book was followed by a letter such as this one.[59]

December, 1897
Mr. Cardley,
I sent you for inspection a copy of a very peculiar book that I want you to see before the edition is exhausted.

I know that you will be glad to see it. If not wanted simply return it by express collect at your convenience and as you are a booklover I'd like to have your criticisms on this work.

With all good wishes and

Sincerely yours ever
Roycroft.

This letter is handwritten and is unusual in its signature. Usually Hubbard's name was signed.

Those who responded with payment would receive books until they returned the books or did not pay for books received. It was a good system. Hubbard knew the success rate at Larkin was high and with his growing audience he could afford an infrequent loss. Most people are honest and those who did not want the book would return it and Hubbard would only lose postage.

As the enterprise grew even the postage for unsolicited books would eat too heavily into working capital so catalogs were issued based upon the same mailing list used for The Philistine. The catalogs are works of advertising persuasion carried to high art. The first two were issued in 1898 and shared the same information though different in format. Catalogs were then issued frequently throughout the life of the press.

They were not annuals, since some were brought out twice a year, probably as inventory increased or significant titles were issued. Some catalogs are so close in content that a line by line survey must be made to determine that a cover change is not the only difference. The Roycrofters, incidentally, did issue catalogs identical in content with different covers through the years.

The 1900 catalogs symbolize all that Elbert Hubbard could put into merchandising. There were two catalogs issued that year. The first was the issue bound in suede and the second is similar in format but expanded. They contain fifteen photogravures of Roycroft personnel and campus as well as the books for sale, current and out-of-print. An essay from the New York Independent on the work of the Roycrofters, six pages of examples of letters received "from a few well-known book lovers", ads for The Message to Garcia, Little Journeys and reports of the success of the Roycroft books at auction completed the contents. The catalogs were sold for two dollars a copy.

A further comment on these catalogs. The letters noted above were one of Hubbard's cleverest ploys. Apparently he ordered books sent to well-known personages. They would, in the etiquette of the times, send a flattering acknowledgment and Hubbard would edit these for insertion in catalogs, etc. Some of those responses found in the 1900 catalogs were from Maude Adams, John Hay, Charles Warren Stoddard, Ellen

Terry and one from Queen Victoria's secretary thanking the Roycrofters on behalf of Her Majesty for the books received.

The 1903 catalog was more subtle. Its thirty-two pages offered books for sale not as a publisher's short list catalog but an annotation on each title to its history, production, availability and price. Intermingled with the books annotations were photos of bindings, furniture in situ and Roycroft personalities. There was an essay by Hubbard A Social and Industrial Experiment (self-promotion) and more letters now called Some Extracts from the Letters From the Elect.

This heavy self-promotion did create a larger audience and more product had to be available so the limited edition again became part of the standard offerings.

The furniture, copper and leather shops were set up to augment the printing shop. The printing shop, as we noted earlier, was expanded as the shop entered its period of greatest productivity and popularity-1903/1910.

Since Kinder had established the bindery the regular editions were bound in ooze calf or paper over boards. Ooze calf or suede, was the arty binding of the day and quite popular so the Roycroft shop cannot be accused, as it has, of being the originator of this unfortunate bookbinding material. The paper over boards binding was retained for those customers wisely favoring traditional book bindings. The regular editions sold at $2.00 for the suede and $5.00 for the paper over boards. Modeled leather bindings produced in the leather shop became available after 1904.[60]

There was also a incised leather binding that was (and is) quite handsome. Three-quarter suede or levant leather combined with plain or marbled paper was offered in most titles. The full levant handtooled books were done for many of the titles as "a few" and advertised in the catalogs.

The novelty bindings used by the Roycroft shop are tastefully done. The leather binding done for The Doctors fits the overall design style while the suede version of the same title is dull. Parchment was used for several titles as the special binding though there is some evidence that in offerings such as The Last Ride it could be considered the regular binding. The shop offered the Alicia binding which was stamped three quarter leather and the Repousse, which was the full modeled leather.

Various dyed or special leathers appear randomly through the offerings as these materials were experimented within the bindery. It is a challenge to try to determine if these odd bindings were singular or part of special offering not noted in the catalogs. Those "different" leather bindings that have been examined in limited editions seem to be part of the normal numbering sequence and were probably just put into the shipping area when finished at the bindery.

The tooled three-quarter or full leather bindings done at the shop are of excellent quality. Those by Louis Kinder are superior to all but any of the Roycroft special bindings are without serious fault in design or craftsmanship. The three-quarter bindings started at $10.00 while the full levant hand tooled bindings were priced from $50. 00 to $250. 00 and sold well at those prices.

Illumination, which was really just filling in the printed decorative initials and borders, also added to the revenues. Illustration, which was hand rendering of the initial letters as well as creation of water-color vignettes was very popular and another excellent seller. These illustrated books were signed by the individual illustrators whereas the illumined were just knocked off on an assembly line basis.

These added attractions together with the expanding demand for the regular offerings added up to a successful business.

The ledger referred to earlier gives us some sales figures for that period 1909-10. For example, the ledger shows that 30,762 copies of *Health and Wealth* were mailed out between September 15 and October 31, 1908 in the United States only. These were, according to the heading "On Inspection" which was the old "On Suspicion" only now the books went to former customers only. A mailing of statements requesting payment for the book was started on January 8, 1909 and 12,224 had been posted by February 2 and the whole statement mailing completed by March. The ledger also gives us some of the production figures for this title. Example of a two day work period shows:

Received	To Stock	Wrapped	Stamp	Mailed
9/8 925	12	913	- *	x
9/17 950	50	900	900	900

It would appear that the books finished each day were sent from the bindery to the shipping area for immediate order filling. The few sent to stock on these average days indicates a tremendous volume of daily sales just for this one Elbert Hubbard title.

Another Hubbard title, *White Hyacinths*, shows us sales figures. On

February 16, 1908, 1,141 copies were mailed; 1,265 on the17th; 1,266 on the 18th and 1,153 on the 19th. At an average of 1,273 copies of this title mailed per day and accepting a five day work week we have 25,460 copies mailed out in one month. The title first appears in the 1907/08 catalog and although its appearance in this biennial catalog suggests a late 1907 publication date we can assume that a total sales of over 100,000 copies is not unreasonable.

The *East Aurora Advertiser* for the week of November 7,1907 stated that the shop was sending out an average of 2,500 packages daily and had about 200,000 books and calendars to ship before Christmas. Even if the Roycrofters had given the newspapers figures inflated by 100% they were doing a healthy amount of business.

What did it cost to produce the books and magazines? Again our one ledger provides some figures.

The shop was paying .1 1 per foot for sheep skins of five to eight foot in various dye colors. Morocco in three to five square foot pieces was .15 per foot while ooze calf in six to eight foot sections was .25 to .28 per carton. Levant in seven to eight foot squares was $65.00 per dozen pieces. India cow hide was .28 for thirty-two to forty square foot sections. They paid $1.10 per yard for silk used for the suede inner linings and .12 per yard for the silk ribbons used in the same suede bindings. There are, unfortunately, no paper nor labor figures in this ledger but we can break down the production costs for one issue of The Fra noted separately in the ledger. Based on a press run of 50,000 we have this breakdown:

Paper stock	$1890.
Composition	100.
Press work	300.
Postage	250.
Express	1,270.

Total expenses were $3,180 or 7.62 cents per copy. The dealers got the issue for 15.5 cents and the subscribers for 17 cents so the shop saw a profit of at least one hundred percent excluding advertising revenue per issue. Sales of the books also showed a steady profit especially in the better bindings. The production process was apparently to print the edition, do the regular binding run and then set the unbound sheets aside for the special binding offerings and orders. Since the press run was paid for by the regular printing, the binding orders could be pro-rated in the bindery. The prices realized were $25 to $250 for a full hand tooled levant binding by Louis Kinder, $10 for a modeled leather binding and the same price for the Alicia, vellum, etc. How much profit did the Roycroft shop get from a binding? Our ledger gives one example. A 1899 Rubaiyat was bound in hand tooled levant and sold for $100. The skins cost $65 per dozen or $5.42 each. This book took one skin and nine hours binding time. If they only paid the binder $1 per hour the cost would be $14.42 plus basis cost of the unbound but sewn book. Doubling the binders wages would still allow a good profit. Another point to consider is that some of the basic binding would be done by the journeymen or even student binders and only the hand tooling or finishing would be done by Kinder.

Other figures available show the profit margin in the other "added attractions" of Roycroft. Stevenson's Prayer, which I assumed is a motto sheet I haven't seen or a special order was charged out at $2 per hundred initials drawn at four minutes each. The shop could hand color the head and tail bands in the illuminated editions at $9 per hundred and do each in two minutes. The photogravure work done at the shop was charged out at $12.50 per plate (and the plate work may have always been done in Buffalo), labor of impressing at $15 per thousand impressions and the Japan Vellum bought at $4.50 to $5.00 per thousand sheets. We can assume that these figures refer to full sheets (25" x 38") and these sheets would give at least a dozen pages per sheet. The intaglio shop was located in the tower and was used not only to produce the photogravures for the little journeys and frontispiece illustrations but for the book plate commissions solicited by the shop. These bookplates were charged out at an average of $25 per design plus printing.

What did it all add up to? A fifteen month survey from April 1909 to June 1910 shown below give the monthly sales figures. It also shows the seasonality of sales that somewhat corroborates the Advertiser story.

April	$43,073.04
May	$28,399.57
June	$30,835.93
July	$14,355.02
August	$14,203.21
September	$20,836.39
October	$34,340.39
November	$33,161.57
December	$40,608.15

| January | $32,585.74 |

The total for the fifteen months was $405,817.26. We cannot confirm this figure as total sales for all of the shops or just the printing shop but since all of the figures so far in the ledger relate to the printing shop a strong assumption can be made that we are looking at printing shop revenues only.

These sums added to the other sources of income such as the furniture shop, metal shop and inn should have given the Hubbards a handsome income. In fact, the Hubbards were going broke. Nancy Hubbard Brady, granddaughter of Elbert and daughter of Bert told of her father being handed a travelers bag full of cash at the end of Hubbard's lecture tours. He was accepting speaking engagements to meet the payroll.[60] We don't have hard evidence of the expenses of the shops but they had to be considerable. One of the office staff[62] estimated that there could have been five hundred employees around 1914 and she remembers spending two days each week helping to fill the pay envelopes. And if there were still large mortgage payments on the equipment and the buildings there could easily have been a cash flow problem.

The one piece of good circumstantial evidence of the monetary difficulties of the enterprise is the action of Bert Hubbard after the death of his parents. He immediately sold the rights of his father's Little Journey and other serial materials to William Wise and Company.

THE END

The sudden deaths of Alice and Elbert left their heir, Elbert ll, with an overextended and inflated business. Once it had been confirmed beyond a doubt that the senior Hubbards were lost Bert had to take immediate stock of the future of the shops. The Roycroft idea was Elbert Hubbard's and he was Roycroft to most of those who had supported the enterprise. Bert had no illusions about his taking his father's place. He was an organizer, not an originator. If Roycroft was to survive it would have to make some radical changes.

Aside from the great personal loss, Bert had to assess the financial loss. How much had the very existence of Elbert Hubbard, writer, lecturer and friend of the powerful brought into the coffers and what could make up that revenue if it was all lost? What about the payroll; who would be kept and who would be released? He would be balancing loyalty against productivity. What could be kept of the past and what could not be kept and for what reasons? A lot of problems faced Bert Hubbard and one that had to be solved had once been a great asset.

Elbert Hubbard had started "The American Academy of Immortals" to do for the books what "The Society of the Philistines" had done for The Philistine subscriptions. "The American Academy of Immortals" cost $10 for a ninety-nine year membership. New members could select $10 worth of books from a select back list for the price of the shipping plus they received all back numbers of The Philistine and Little Journeys for the year of their joining and all that would be published for the next ninety-nine years.

The Life Memberships gave the member all of the above plus a discount on furniture. The member's obligations were, if possible, to attend The Pastor's (Hubbard) lectures for one dollar per seat, buy Roycroft furniture and consider Roycroft books as the perfect gift.

Later the Thirty-Third Degree was added. This cost $125 and would give the respondent $125 worth of "richly bound" Roycroft books. In addition to these books, the Thirty-Third Degree member would receive one copy free of every title published by the shop for the rest of the member's life. Further inducement was a gift of the Roycroft furniture listed on a sheet enclosed with the membership or from selected furniture ads in The Philistines or The Fra. Freight charges would be the member's only cost. This scheme had been very helpful to Elbert Hubbard during the expansion period of the press. It had raised considerable money and reduced the inventory of back issues of the magazines and slow selling books. Plus the furniture was going out of vogue so it got rid of that. Now Bert was faced with a commitment that could bankrupt the shop and/or cause trouble with those Life and Thirty-Third Degree members who would not care for the commercial titles he proposed to print and would want furniture from the shop he wanted to close. He also knew there would be no new member for the "American Academy of Immortals" without Elbert Hubbard so all members received this letter.

October 7, 1916

My dear Thirty-Thirder:
You were my father's staunch friend. You helped him to make the Roycroft Shop a success. He was your friend too, I know. More than a year ago he left East Aurora on his last Little Journey. He left an institution here for me to perpetuate. It is my duty to play fair and square. Years ago you became a Thirty-Third Degree Roycrofter, which subject I wish to discuss with you.

For many reasons I find it almost imperative to clear up these "perpetual" contracts. And I need your help. I find that under this arrangement you have received considerably more than your original investment, and I want you to receive more, but instead of sending you books over a period of years I want to give you extra value now, and ask you to release us from the Thirty-Third agreement.

I submit this proposition to you. On the enclosed blanks are listed a number of extra choice deluxe books. These books my father printed and personally supervised. They will not be reproduced or duplicated. Already they have become rare and they will increase in value as time goes on.

If you select and check off on the enclosed blank any five and sign the release, I will ship these books to you by express prepaid. As Christmas gifts they will come in handy, provided you don't need them for your own library. I know these exquisite volumes will more than please you, and to clear up these old contracts will solve a perplexing problem and mightily help us with our business arrangements here.

Apparently he got out of the contracts.

The shop continued on into the Depression, but after 1915 they were a commercial printer that issued reprints of some of the Elbert Hubbard titles plus more vanity printing. They had the printing contracts for the Hubbard material sold to Wise & Co. This was a good source of business but they only saw what they got for the printing and Wise & Co. got what money the name of Elbert Hubbard could still generate.

The shop closed in 1935. The buildings and equipment changed hands several times before closing for good in 1942.

Before we start the Bibliography we must address one charge always laid against the Roycrofters and Elbert Hubbard. Were the limited editions really limited? The charge was made in Elbert's time and is still made today. It is a true charge in many cases as will be shown in the next chapter.

Is He Sincere?

ARE THEY REAL?

W. W. Denslow's cartoon visualizes a question raised often during Elbert Hubbard's tenure as Fra Elbertus. The question is: Are They Real? Are the limited editions really limited? What was the motivation behind others signing Hubbard's name in the limitation statements? Did the Roycrofters make any attempt to define editions?

The Roycroft Press has always suffered suspicion from collectors, librarians and dealers both in its limited and regular editions. The more serious accusations concern the limited editions.

The question of the signed and limited Roycroft editions being truly limited is important not only from a bibliographical point of view but as a matter of ethics and personal morality - two virtues expounded by Hubbard.

I have no concrete evidence to condemn nor vindicate the Roycroft Press of the charges of duplicity that have plagued it, but I will offer evidence as I have collected it.

Taber[63] stated that the *Song of Songs* went through four printings and that later editions could be distinguished by the omission of his name from the colophon. There is no evidence to support Mr. Taber. I have examined more than one dozen copies of this book, both in the regular and limited edition and his name has appeared in all copies. I have observed no variation or "points" in any of those copies I have examined. I will say that all of the copies that I have examined were in Western New York collections.

What about true limitation? Let's start with a conversation that supposedly took place between Elbert Hubbard and Charles Everitt, rare book dealer and reported in Everitt's book *Adventures of a Treasure Hunter*.[64]

"Mr. Hubbard, you put out a book recently in an edition strictly limited to a hundred copies. So far, I have personally seen a hundred fifteen copies. How about it?" Hubbard grinned, "Oh, those are limited to a hundred copies for each state."

This conversation may or may not have taken place. There are several points against Everitt in this story. He reports that the conversation took place several days before Hubbard sailed and went down on the Titanic. Hubbard lost his life on the Lusitania. Also, how did Everitt see so many copies of one edition? Mostly all of the Roycroft books were mailed directly to the customers. Whatever, it is stories such as this that have made dealers and librarians shy away from the Roycroft books as valid-collectable items of a press and a period.

What evidence is there for duplicity? I can offer the following information.

The only bibliographical sources for Roycroft books have been the catalogs of the press and Albert Lane's *Elbert Hubbard and His Work* [65]The catalogs abound with error and contradiction. Books were supposed to have been issued on a certain paper stock and bound in a distinct style but the book is actually printed on a different stock and offered in a binding not mentioned in the catalog. The edition numbers seem to have been invented. One can assume that Lane got his information from East Aurora and hence they did not know how many they were issuing or chose to give false information.

Here are some examples:

Lane noted 750 copies of *The Journal of Koheleth*. The limited statement in the book gives 700 as the edition number.

352 copies in the limiting statement of *Art and Life*. Lane notes 350 copies, bound in limp chamois; 100 specially bound in paper over boards and 100 specially illumined. A specially illumined copy examined states 109 copies.

Lane notes 920 copies of *On Going to Church* done on hand made paper with a numbered and decorated edition of 25 copies on Tokyo Vellum. The edition has no limiting statement.

Lane notes 500 copies for *Glynne's Wife*. The statement in the book shows 596 copies and The Philistine of December 1896 advertises 590 copies.

Lane notes 500 copies of *Upland Pastures*. The limiting statement in the book shows 600 copies. There was also supposed to be an edition of 40 copies printed on Japan Vellum and illumined by Bertha Hubbard. None of this special edition has been located.

In the *Track of the Bookworm* shows 590 copies in its limiting statement. Lane notes 500 copies.

Lane notes 300 copies of *The Book of Job* while the book shows 350 copies in the limiting statement. Copies 1-40 were supposed to be specially illumined but several of these low numbers have been found without illumination and two copies with higher numbers were illuminated.

A catalog ad of 1898 calls for 480 copies of *The Sonnets from the Portuguese*. Lane notes 425. The limitation statement in copies examined shows 480.

Lane notes an edition of 600 for *Love Letters of a Musician*. Copies examined have a limiting statement showing 900 and those limiting statements are in "error" in stating that the initial letters are hand drawn. Every copy examined has printed initial letters.

Lane shows 925 copies for *IN MEMORIAM* while the 1898 catalog call for 910. This number agrees with the limiting statement in the books.

The Dipsy Chanty has a limiting statement of 100 copies specially illumined. The catalog for the year of issue notes [66] specially illumined which agrees with Lane's figure.

Essays of Elia has two interesting discrepancies. Lane and the books examined agree on the edition number - 970. The 1898 catalog notes 900 copies. The second discrepancy is the date of publication. The books examined show a 1899 date but two privately prepared check lists now in the Elbert Hubbard Museum show 1898 and 1898/99 as the dates for the books in those collections. This point is unresolved at time of publication.

The Ancient Mariner is advertised as 900 copies in a regular edition with 400 specially illumined and 40 copies on Japan Vellum. The actual copies examined show 910 as the limiting figure and there is no evidence to support the limited editions though no doubt they do exist in some number.

Sonnets of Shakespeare shows 980 as the limiting number in copies examined while Lane calls for 900 and a contemporary catalog agrees with Lane.

The Intellectual Life states 960 copies in examples; Lane notes 950.

Lane states 500 copies of *The Deserted Village* were issued with 5 specially illumined. A 1898 catalog calls for 470 copies which agrees with the limiting statements of the books but calls for 9 specially illumined copies. One additional note on this title. All sources of reference noted above call for Whatman Hand Made as the paper stock. My copy, 20/470 is printed on Dickinson.

This inconsistency continues throughout the comparison of Lane, the catalogs and the actual books. Which is correct? Who knows.

Duplication is not easily proved in limited editions, however, there are now two cases that may prove duplication. I still emphasize the "may".

I have in my own collection two copies of *The City of Tagaste*: one copy is numbered 214 and the other 929 of an edition of 940. The limiting statement of one copy reads: "Of this edition on Hand Made Paper there were printed and specially hand illumined nine hundred and forty copies, and this book is No. 214." The limiting statement of the other reads: "Of this edition there were printed and specially illumined nine hundred and forty copies, and this book is Number 929. " The numbers are pen written and both copies are signed in Elbert Hubbard's name. One is illumined by Harriat Robarge and the other by Minnie Gardner. Both copies are identical in format, paper stock, binding, etc. No readily observable "points" are present. The only difference are the wording in the limiting statements and that the limiting statement of one copy is a four page signature sewn in while the other limitation statement is part of the standard sixteen page signature. What happened? Are these two copies from the only edition or was there more than one edition? The different signature make-up could be explained. The copy with the four page introductory signatures could have had a damaged sixteen page form and in resetting the type the book could have been reformatted to finish the press run for the one and only edition. In remaking the form someone could have changed the wording of the limitation statement unknowingly. It could happen. Or, there were editions for every state as Hubbard supposedly told Mr. Everitt. Whatever, it is the closest case of duplication that I have uncovered to this point.

Jay T. Johnson, a book dealer in Los Angeles has a new duplication to report. He has two copies of the 1899 *Essay on Friendship* both numbered 45 or an edition of 50.Both are specially illumined and signed by Clara Schlegel. Fraud? Perhaps of just someone in the shop who lost count. Remember that the employers who did the numbering (and signing Elbert Hubbard's name) were often schoolgirls with little thought of the implications of their afterschool work.

The regular editions of the Roycroft imprints were not numbered and must be excluded from this investigation. The only area of duplication would be in those volumes advertised as specially illumined or bound. As to the differences in makeup of one title that can be explained in the way the books were marketed. The shop would produce a run of one title and bind a percentage. The rest of the press run would be stored as uncollated sheets. These would be used for the special illumination and binding offerings. If the title proved to be very popular and was sold out as the shop loved to advertise in the catalogs it would be reset and offered again. One will find the popular titles with several variants in paper stock, type face and decoration as well as binding. Since these were not advertised as "special" only the exclusion of the printing history of the title can be held against the shop. That is serious enough but I really don't think they were aware of the importance of that statement in a book.

In summation, the question is one of integrity. Throughout this history there has been one instance after another of Elbert Hubbard's unethical treatment of others. As to the limited editions, the treatment of the signature proves to me that Elbert Hubbard was in it for the money.

A signature in a limiting statement is an attestation. One can believe that what is stated in the limitation statement is the truth. Here the limitations statements were not even signed by the person attesting to the truth of that statement. The examples given in plate two show the variation found in a survey. They are compared with a signature known to be made by Elbert Hubbard. If one sold a limited edition today and asked a premium price because it was signed by Elbert Hubbard and it wasn't, what is the law on that situation? Fraud? I don't blame those who actually signed the books years ago because they were naive and were told to do so as part of their employment. Elbert Hubbard was just a sharp businessman whose promotional background gave him a distorted set of ethics. P. T. Barnum would have understood Elbert Hubbard.

I wish I could have been kinder to Elbert Hubbard in this study. I don't feel that he was an unkind or dishonest man. I don't feel that he was anything but a man of his class and time. His kindness will be weighed against his work and will be found wanting.

THE BIBLIOGRAPHY
1896
1. ART AND LIFE
By Vernon Lee (Violet Paget)
8¾" x 5⅜" 91 pages.
Body copy set in Old Style Antique.
352 copies printed in two colors on Japan Vellum and bound in suede. 109 copies bound in paper over boards with cloth spine. 12 copies specially illumined by W. W. Denslow. 10 copies were specially illumined by William B. Favrile. (Favrile was a friend from Hubbard's Boston days). All copies of the book were numbered and signed by Bertha Hubbard.

2. FOREIGN IDEAS IN THE CATHOLIC CHURCH IN AMERICA
By Father George Zurcher
9 ¹⁄₁₆" x 5¾" 56 pages.
Body copy set in Caslon.
Roycroft Quarterly number three, November 1896. Last of the Roycroft Quarterlies.

3. GLYNNE'S WIFE
By Julia Ditto Young
6⅛" x 4½" 143 pages.
Body copy set in Caslon.
596 copies printed on Ruisdael handmade paper with limitation page printed on Japan Vellum. Bound in Silk over boards. 25 copies on Tokyo Vellum hand decorated by author. Entire issue was numbered and signed by author.

4. JOURNAL OF KOHELETH, THE
Being a reprint of the Book of Ecclesiastes with an essay by Elbert Hubbard.
9⅛" x 6⅛" 76 pages
Body copy set in Old Style Antique.
Printed in two colors, red and black, in an edition of 700 copies on Ruisdael. Bound on paper over boards with cloth spine. 12 copies printed on Japan Vellum. Bound in paper over boards with cloth spine. Title page designed by Bertha Hubbard and the edition numbered and signed by Elbert Hubbard. This is the second book issued by the press and there are numerous variant bindings including those copies bound in cloth ties.

5. LEGACY, THE
A Novel by Elbert Hubbard in two volumes.
6⅞" x 4½" 448 pages.
Body copy set in Caslon.
900 copies (Lane) printed on Dickinson Dekel-Edge and bound in suede.

Frontispiece paper photogravure of Elbert Hubbard with title page in two colors on Japan Vellum.

6. ON GOING TO CHURCH
By George Bernard Shaw
6⅞" x 4½" 40 pages.
Body copy set in Old Style Antique.
Lane notes 420 copies printed on Dickinson Dekel-Edge and bound in paper over boards with white cloth spine. He also notes an edition of 25 copies printed on Tokyo Vellum and decorated with water colors by Bertha Hubbard. All of this information appears in an ad in the September 1896 Philistine except the limitation number of the regular edition. This ad also states that the vellum edition is sold out. We cannot verify the limitation figures given above as the regular edition is not limited nor signed and we have not seen any copies of the vellum edition. There are, however, variant editions of this book and they are noted below. The points are the make up of the title page, cover and use of colors. Minor points are the color of the cover stock and colophon treatment.
a. (variant one)
Title page reads:
THIS IS THE PREACHMENT (3 ornaments) ON GOING TO CHURCH (3 orn)
WRIT BY GEORGE BERNARD SHAW
AND DONE INTO PRINT AT THE
ROYCROFT PRINTING SHOP (orn) WHICH IS IN EAST AURORA,
NEW YORK, U.S.A. (3 ornaments) MDCCCXCVI
(Roycroft mark here in red)
Binding is light gray paper over boards or dark gray paper over boards. Both covers have white cloth spine. Cover copy is On Going to Church (acorn), in gold stamped roman type.
b. (variant two)
THIS IS THE PREACHMENT
ON GOING TO CHURCH, WRIT BY GEORGE BERNARD SHAW
& DONE INTO PRINT AT THE ROYCROFT PRINTING SHOP WHICH IS IN
EAST AURORA ERIE CO., NEW YORK, U.S.A. MDCCCXCVI
(Roycroft mark here in black)
Binding is dark gray paper over boards with half suede spine. Title copy on cover is set: On Going to Church (Gothic); SHAW, centered below (Roman).
c. (variant three)
ON GOING TO CHURCH: (in red)
Being the Preachment which (rest of title in black) treats of Church-Going, Art, and Some Other Themes (orn) (orn) by George Bernard Shaw (Roycroft mark in red and
Done into a book at the Roycroft Shop which is in East Aurora
New York, U.S.A.
MDCCCXCVI
Binding is dark gray paper over boards with white cloth spine. Cover type is ON GOING TO CHURCH set in roman caps and small caps. Shaw's name is omitted.

7. RUSKIN-TURNER
By Elbert Hubbard
10" x 7¾" 53 pages.
Body copy set in Old Style Antique.
473 copies printed on Whatman handmade paper and bound in paper over
boards with cloth spine or bound in suede with cloth ties. 26 copies printed on
Japan Vellum, hand illumined by Bertha Hubbard and bound in crushed levant.
Both editions illustrated with photogravures of Turner's work on vellum; numbered and signed in Elbert Hubbard's name.There are supposedly specially illumined copies. These and any special bindings are unexamined at this time.

8. SONG OF SONGS, THE
Reprinted from the Song of Songs, with an introductory essay by Elbert
Hubbard
9⅛" X 6" 72 pages.
Body copy set in Old Style Antique.
600 copies printed on Ruisdael; bound in paper over boards with cloth spine.
12 copies printed on Japan Vellum; bound in paper over boards with cloth
spine.Both editions have a two color title page designed by Bertha Hubbard.
Both editions are numbered and signed by Elbert Hubbard.This is the first book
of the press. There is an ad in the December 1895 Philistine that specifies
Dickinson paper for this book and notes the binding as flexible Japan Vellum.
We have seen no copies that fit these specifications. As noted earlier, Harry
Taber asserted that there were several editions of this work and the later printings can be ascertained by the absence of his name in the colophon. His claim
has no supporting evidence.

9. SOUVENIR AND A MEDLEY, A
Seven poems and a sketch by Stephen Crane
7½" x 5¼" 48 pages.
Body copy set in Old Style Antique.
Roycroft Quarterly number one. Paper bound. May 1896. Press run unknown.

10. THIS THEN IS THE PREACHMENT ON GOING TO CHURCH
By George Bernard Shaw
7¼" x 4¾" 40 pages.
Body copy set in Old Style Antique.
Paper bound. Roycroft Quarterly number two. August 1896. Press run unknown
but presumably issued before the hard bound editions.

1897
11. BOOK OF JOB, THE
As translated from the Original by Rabbi Abraham Elzas; With Some Comments
on the Poem by Elbert Hubbard
7¾" x 4⅞" 142 pages.
Body copy set in Old Style Antique.
350 copies printed on Whatman handmade paper; hand illumined. The first 40
copies were specially hand illumined by Bertha Hubbard. Complete edition

bound in paper over boards with cloth spine. Numbered and signed by Elbert Hubbard. Four copies are known to be bound in full levant.

12. HOT STUFF
By A. W. Mack
5" x 8" 12 pages.
Body copy set in Old Style Antique.
A fun edition of 13 copies printed on cut-offs of Whatman. The frontispiece reads: "Of this Book there were printed only thirteen copies (for luck) - the Printers were then annihilated, and this volume is no.   ." The title page continues the jest. "This Incomparable Book is Hot Stuff from the pen of that Poet, Prophet and Wit (Big Lewis) - Done into a book at the instigation of his enemy, A. W. Mack." The books were illustrated by W. W. Denslow and Elizabeth Stearns.

13. IN THE TRACK OF THE BOOK-WORM
Essays by Irving Browne
8¾" x 5½" 135 pages.
Body copy set in Old Style Antique. Regular edition of 590 copies printed in two colors on Boxmoor paper. 25 copies printed on Whatman. Both editions were bound in paper over boards, hand illumined by Roycroft artists and numbered and signed by the author.

14. LOVE BALLADS OF THE XVI CENTURY A collection of unsigned poems
8⅛" x 5" 120 pages.
Preface set in Monotype Series 16.
Body copy set in Old Style Antique.
Printed in two colors on Ruisdael and bound in paper over boards with cloth spine. 40 copies specially hand illumined; most copies of this book have some initial letter illumination. Press run unknown.

15. ON THE HEIGHTS
A Volume of Verse by Lucius Harwood Foote
8⅝" x 5⅜" 121 pages.
Body copy set in Old Style Antique.
500 copies printed on unmarked laid paper in two colors. Edition bound in boards with cloth back strip. Printed for the California Guild of Letters.
The only Roycroft publication with an errata sheet.

16. SESAME AND LILIES
By John Ruskin
7¾" X 4⅞" 142 pages.
Body copy set in Old Style Antique.
450 copies printed in two colors on Whatman; hand illumined.
40 copies specially hand illumined.
Binding was paper over boards with white cloth spine. Copies were bound in 3/4 and full levant. The complete edition was numbered and signed by Elbert Hubbard.

17. STORY OF SAVILLE, THE
By Julia Ditto Young
8¾" X 5½" 101 pages.
Body copy set in Caslon.
400 copies printed in two colors on unmarked laid paper. 10 copies specially illumined. Binding was paper over boards with cloth spine. Numbered and signed by the author.

18. UPLAND PASTURES
Essays by Adeline Knapp
8" x 5" 61 pages
Body copy set in Old Style Antique
Regular edition of 600 copies printed in two colors on Ruisdael with title page printed on Japan Vellum. Numbered and signed by Elbert Hubbard.
40 copies printed on Japan Vellum. Hand illumined and signed by Bertha Hubbard. Regular binding was paper over boards with cloth and paper spine. Copies were available in 3/4 and full levant. The edition was also available with hand illumination by Roycroft artists.

1898
19. AS IT SEEMS TO ME
By Elbert Hubbard
8⅝" x 5½" 138 pages.
Body copy set in Old Style Antique.
920 copies printed in two colors on Boxmoor with frontispiece portrait of Hubbard on Japan Vellum. Bound in suede with two cover designs. 40 copies printed on Whatman and specially illumined. Numbers 1 through 4 of this issue were decorated by W. W. Denslow. These four copies are supposed to have thirty-five original water color sketches and decorated initials. None have been found for confirmation. Bindings exist in 3/4 and full levant. These would be later rebindings.

20. CONFESSIONS OF AN OPIUM-EATER
By Thomas De Quincy
8⅝" x 5½" 188 pages.
Body copy set in Old Style Antique.
925 copies printed in two colors on Boxmoor with Lombardic initials embellished in gold. Bound in paper over boards with suede spine. Numbered and signed in Elbert Hubbard's name.There is an interesting variant here. Roycroft covers are quite diverse in style but rarely change titles. Here there are two cover titles. One reads: THE OPIUM EATER on the front cover. The other reads: CONFESSIONS OF AN (2 ornaments) OPIUM EATER (ornament). There are no internal differences and no apparent precedence.

21. DESERTED VILLAGE, THE
By Oliver Goldsmith to which is prefaced some notes concerning a Little Journey to "Sweet Auburn" as written by Elbert Hubbard
11¼" X 8⅝" 55 pages.

Body copy in Bookman.
470 copies in two colors on Whatman. Regular edition has hand drawn initial letters with nine copies specially illumined. Bound in paper over boards with cloth spine. Each copy numbered and signed in Elbert Hubbard's name.
170 copies printed on Japan Vellum with nine specially illumined copies; various binding styles employed. *See Are They Real? for discrepancies noted on this volume.*

22. DIPSY CHANTY, THE
And Other Selected Poems By Rudyard Kipling
8" x 5" 90 pages.
Body copy set in Old Style Antique.
950 copies printed in three colors on Van Gelder handmade paper and bound in suede. Some copies were bound in suede with sterling silver corners.
100 copies specially illumined. All copies were supposedly numbered and signed by Elbert Hubbard but we have seen unnumbered and unsigned copies. The 1898 catalog calls for only 60 specially illumined copies. We suspect the special illumination was only hand embellishment of the Lombardic initial letters with gold.

23. DREAM OF JOHN BALL, A
Essay by William Morris
8¾" x 5⅜" 147 pages.
Body copy set in Old Style Antique.
650 copies printed in two colors on Boxmoor and bound in paper over boards with cloth spine. 100 copies printed on Whatman and bound in paper over boards with cloth spine.

24. FLUSH OF JUNE
By Marcia Bradbury Jordan
5½" x 4¼" 105 pages.
Body copy set in Old Style Antique.
Printed in two colors, black and orange, on Boxmoor and bound in suede. Edition limited to 500 copies. We have only examined one copy of this work; it was numbered but unsigned. No other information is available.

25. HAND AND BRAIN
A Symposium of Essays on Applied Socialism by William Morris, Grant Allen, George Bernard Shaw, Henry S. Salt, Alfred Russel Wallace and Edward Carpenter
9¼" x 5¾" 142 pages.
Body copy set in Old Style Antique.
720 copies printed on Kelmscott handmade paper with hand colored initials. Bound in paper over boards with suede or cloth spine. Many copies are numbered but not signed. Completed September 1,1898. Could have been designed by W. W. Denslow.

The Dard Hunter octopus cover that Hubbard accepted for his Standard Oil defensive essay.

THE SONG OF SONGS
WHICH IS SOLOMONS
BEING A REPRINT
AND A STUDY BY
✠✠✠✠ ELBERT HUBBARD

THE ROYCROFT
PRINTING SHOP
MDCCCXCVI ✠✠✠

The title page designed and drawn by Bertha Hubbard. The paper has foxed badly on this first book of the press.

The third book done by the press and the first done under the supervision of Cy Rosen. The improvement is quite obvious.

THE BOOK OF JOB ❦ As
Translated from the Original
by Rabbi Abraham Elzas; with
some Comments on the Poem
by Elbert Hubbard ❦ ❦ ❦ ❦

DONE INTO A BOOK AT THE ROY-
CROFT SHOP WHICH IS IN EAST
AURORA, NEW YORK, U. S. A.
MDCCCXCVII.

T WINDERMERE a good friend told me that I must abandon all hope of seeing Mr. Ruskin; for I had no special business with him, no letters of introduction, and then the fact that I am an American made it final. Americans in England are supposed to pick flowers in private gardens, cut their names on trees, laugh boisterously at trifles, and make invidious comparisons. Very properly Mr. Ruskin does not admire these things

HERE were no visitors about when I arrived and I thought I would have the coffee room all to myself at luncheon time; but presently there came in a pleasant-faced old gentleman in knickerbockers. He bowed to me and then took a place at the table. He said that it was a fine day and I agreed with him, adding that the mountains were very beautiful. He assented, putting in a codicil to the effect that the lake was very pretty. Then the waiter came for our orders

"Together, I s'pose?" remarked Thomas inquiringly, as he halted at the door and balanced the tray on his finger tips.

"Yes, serve lunch for us together," said the ruddy old gentleman as he

The basic filled-in initials that were mass-produced and added much to the profits.

HILE we float here, far from that tributary stream on whose banks our friends and kindred dwell, our thoughts, like the stars, come out of their horizon still; for there circulates a finer blood than Lavoisier has discovered the laws of,—the blood, not of kindred merely, but of kindness, whose pulse still beats at any distance and forever. After years of vain familiarity, some distant gesture or unconscious behavior, which we remember, speaks to us with more emphasis than the wisest or kindest words. We are sometimes made aware of a kindness long passed, and realize that there have been times when our friends' thoughts of us were of so pure and lofty a character that they passed over us like the winds of heaven unnoticed; when they treated us not as what we were, but as what we aspired to be. There has just reached us, it may be, the nobleness of some such silent behavior, not to be forgotten, not to be remembered, and we shudder to think how it fell on us cold, though in some true but tardy hour we endeavor to wipe off these scores. In my experience, persons, when they are made

Illumination. Each decorative initial letter was hand done.

The Song of Songs :
Which is Solomon's.

The binding style of the first Roycroft books. It was done in Buffalo at a trade bindery in imitation of the Kelmscotts.

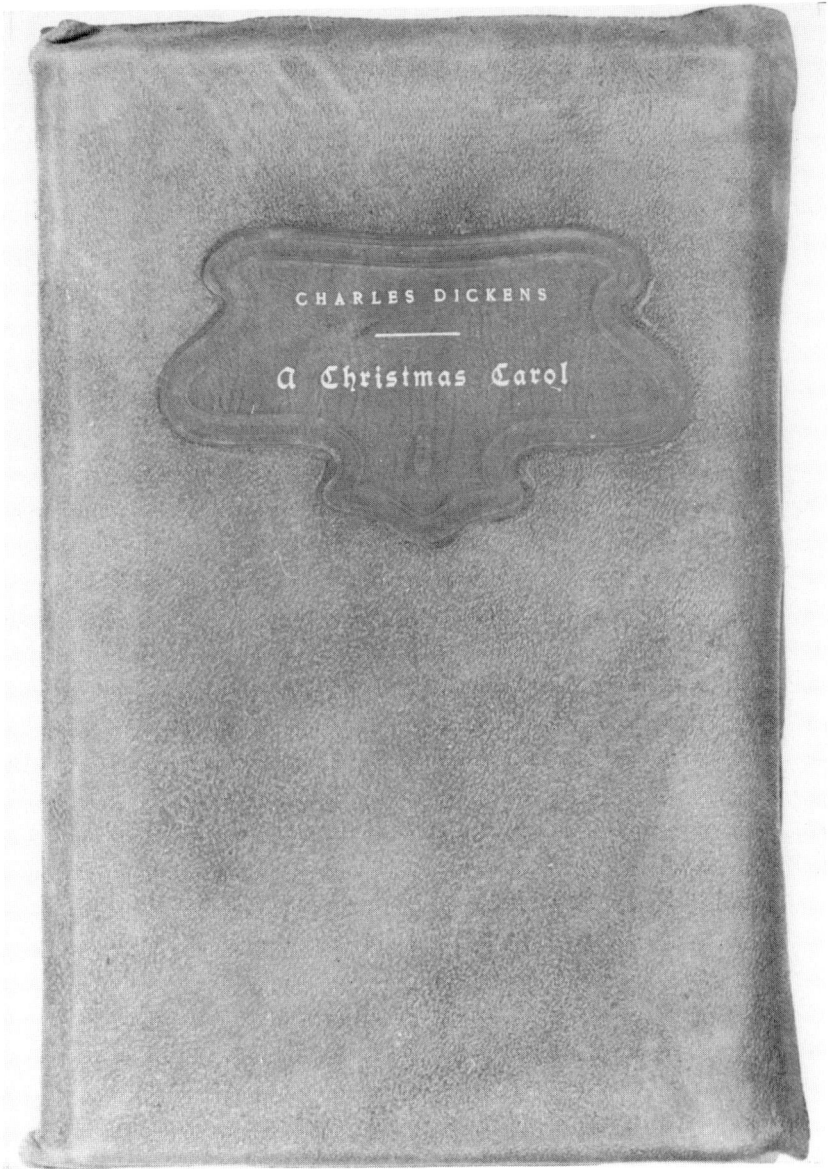

The standard suede binding. Called "window washers" by the binders it was the most popular binding with the average Roycroft customer.

The three-quarter leather which became a standard offering with the shop after Louis Kinder established the bindery.

A Modeled leather binding done in the leather shop.

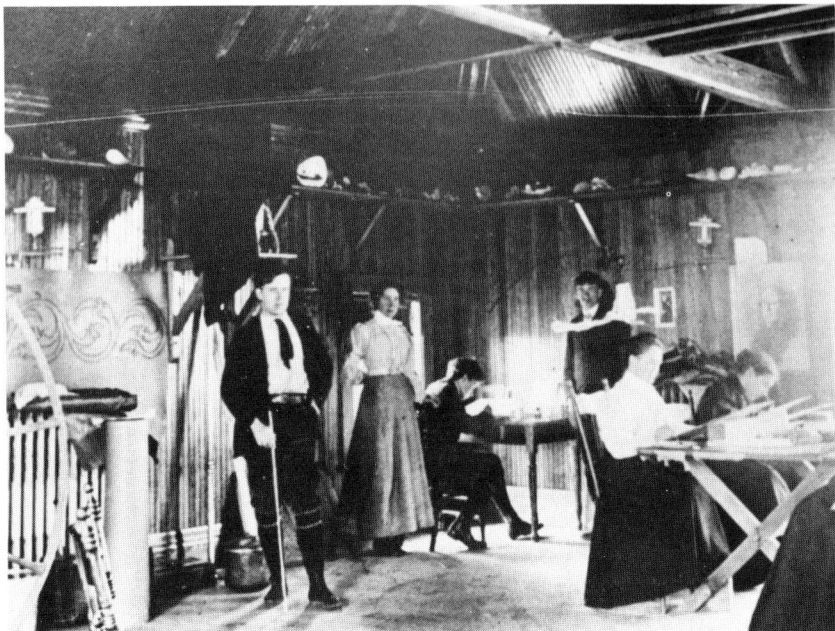

The early illumination studio. Samuel Warner is standing to the left center.

The early bindery showing *The Philistine* magazine being collated and stitched.

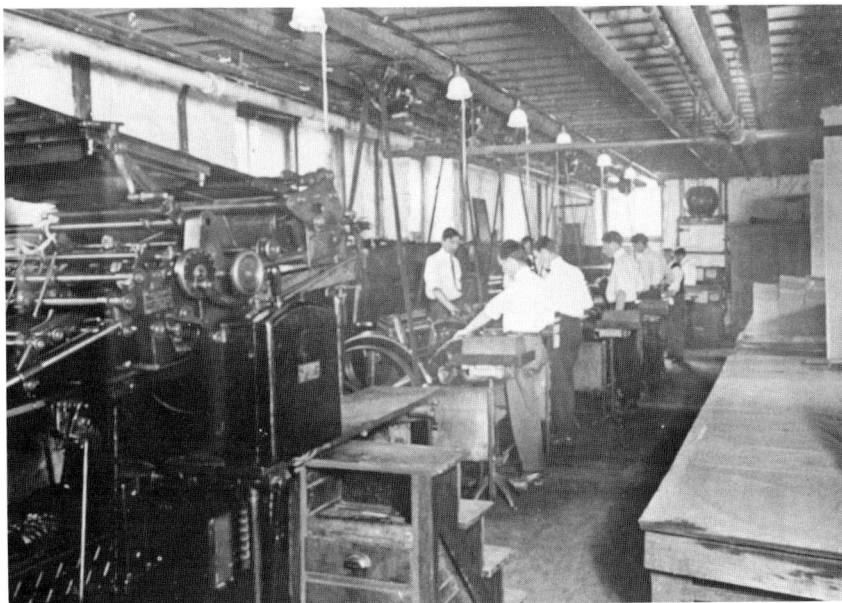

One side of the basement press room showing the Harris press in the foreground and some of the Colt Armoury presses in line.

The print shop as seen from the front on Main Street.

The typesetting and composition area on the first floor of the printing shop. The Washington press acquired as the shop's first press is in the middle of the picture.

Another view of the composition side of the typesetting shop. The paper storage area is in the background.

The Monotype keyboards which were installed in 1903. Below, the Monotype casting units which were in the basement.

The Roycroft baseball team and the Roycroft band below with a young Bert Hubbard (E. H. II) in the foreground.

was weaned. Wrinkled, toothless, yellow old hags are
seen sitting by the roadside, rocking back and forth,

Barnhart Bros & Splinder Old Style Antique

continued habit of pure thinking and simple
living brings a reward beyond the value of

Monotype Cushing

ıly ex- cliques and keep the millenium of lect
a man   Peace and Good-will a very dim and inci
men-   thv

McFarland Series from Inland Type Foundry

hensile, with fingers knotted like a cord;
and they were continually flickering in

Bruce Roman

to warm himself at the candle; in which effort,
not being a man of strong imagination, he failed.

Monotype Caslon Old Style

the intermediary was quite needless
and unnecessary—and worse, it was the

ATF Wayside

POWERFUL Western fallen star!
O shades of night—O moody, tearful night!
O great star disappeared—O the black murk that

Monotype Bookman

have risen from her bed and grasped that
baby to her heart, and given her life to

Monotype Kennerley

Examples of some of the common and uncommon typefaces found in the books.

Variations of Hubbard's signature. The bottom example is the authentic signature. The variations are numerous and quite varied.

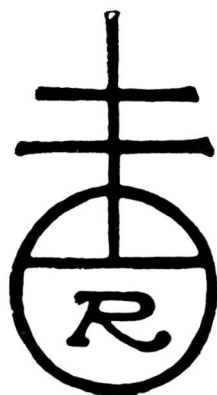

Marks of Dard Hunter, W. W. Denslow and the standard Roycroft mark designed by H. P. Taber; founder of the press.

26. IN MEMORIAM
By Alfred Tennyson
8" x 5" 179 pages.
Body copy set in Old Style Antique.
910 copies printed on Ruisdael with special initial letters in color by Denslow.
General edition binding was suede with some copies bound in 3/4 levant.
Completed August 4,1898.

27. LITTLE JOURNEYS TO THE HOMES OF FAMOUS WOMEN
By Elbert Hubbard
11" x 8⅝"193 pages.
Body copy set in Old Style Antique.
470 copies printed on Dickinson. Initials and paragraph marks inserted in red
and blue ink by hand. Bound in paper over boards.The 1898 catalog notes that
there were about 2,000 paragraph marks in each volume. This would be quite
an effort in hand decoration and illustrative of the industry of the small art staff.

28. LOVE-LETTERS OF A MUSICIAN
By Myrtle Reed
8" x 5" 103 pages.
Body copy set in Old Style Antique.
900 copies printed in two colors on Ruisdael. Editions numbered but not signed.
Bound in suede with blind stamped design and gold stamped typography.
Two discrepancies here. Lane's bibliography notes 600 copies and the two
copies I have inspected have insertions that all initial letters are drawn in by
hand whereas they are obviously printed.

29. RUBAIYAT OF OMAR KHAYYAM, THE
5½" x 7⁵⁄₁₆" 60 pages.
Body copy set in Old Style Antique.
920 copies printed on Boxmoor in three colors and bound in olive green suede.
Initial letters are in alternating red and blue and body copy is in black. Seahorse
appears in colophon. This edition was completed June 10, 1898.
40 copies specially illumined according to catalog.

30. RUBAIYAT OF OMAR KHAYYAM, THE
5⅝" x 9" 67 pages.
Body copy set in Old Style Antique.
670 copies printed in three colors, red, blue and black, on Dickinson paper.
Hand drawn initial letters and bound in suede. Completed November 2, 1898.

31. SERMONS FROM A PHILISTINE PULPIT
By William McIntosh (Doctor Phil)
5¾" x 4¼" 75 pages.
Body copy set in Old Style Antique.
Printed in two colors on Dickinson and bound in paper over boards with cloth
backstrap.

32. SONNETS FROM THE PORTUGUESE
By Elizabeth Barrett Browning to which is prefaced a Little Journey to the Home of the Author, Written by Elbert Hubbard
11" x 8½" 68 pages.
Body copy set in Old Style Antique.
480 copies printed on Whatman handmade with initials designed by Denslow. Bound in paper over boards with cloth spine. Completed May 13, 1898.

1899
33. ALI BABA OF EAST AURORA
By Fra Elbertus (Elbert Hubbard)
7⅝" x 5½" 150 pages.
Body copy set in Caslon Old Style.
620 copies printed in three colors on Roycroft handmade paper. 26 copies printed on Imperial Japan Vellum. The editions were signed with an (X) and signature by "Ali Baba". Some copies of the regular and limited editions were hand illumined and signed by the illuminator. All copies have photogravure portrait of Blackman as frontispiece.
Bindings were suede, boards with suede spine, half morocco and probable 3/4 and full leather.

34. ANCIENT MARINER, THE
By Samuel Taylor Coleridge
8¾" x 5⅝" 140 pages.
Body copy set in Caslon Old Style.
910 copies printed on handmade paper in three colors with initial letters and 14 pseudo-woodcuts by W. W. Denslow. Text printed in red and black with illustrations in green. 400 copies specially illumined. 40 copies specially illumined and printed on Japan Vellum. Binding was decorated suede. There are cover design variants for this book in the suede binding and two copies on Japan Vellum are known to have been bound full Levant.

35. AUCASSIN AND NICOLETTE
Translated by Andrew Lang
8" x 5⅛" 91 pages.
Body copy set in Old Style Antique.
940 copies printed on Roycroft handmade paper. 25 copies printed on Imperial handmade paper. Both editions bound in suede. One copy known to be bound full levant. Advertising notes all copies are "hand lettered", but this is nothing more than hand coloring of printed initial letters.

36. BALLADS OF A BOOK-WORM
By Irving Browne
8¼" x 5½" 120 pages.
Body copy set in Old Style Antique.
850 copies printed on Whatman handmade paper. 31 copies printed on Japan Vellum. All copies have hand illumined title page and initial letters. Bound in paper over boards with paper labels. Limiting statement numbered and signed

in Elbert Hubbard's name. Completed April 21, 1899.

37. BIGOTRY BACILLUS, THE
By Elbert Hubbard
8⅝" x 5⅜" 17 pages.
Body copy set in Old Style Antique.
Printed on unmarked laid paper with hand drawn initials. Bound in brown cover stock. Press run unknown.

38. CHRISTMAS EVE
By Robert Browning with a study of the poem by Mary H. Hull
7⅞" x 5½" 81 pages
Body copy set in Old Style Antique.
Regular edition printed in one color on Boxmoor and bound in suede. Many hand illumined initial copies will be found.
50 copies printed on Japan Vellum and bound in suede. Some of these are also hand illumined and some were bound in hand tooled vellum.

39. DIPSY CHANTY, THE
By Rudyard Kipling
8¼" x 5" 92 pages.
Body copy set in Old Style Antique.
950 copies printed on unmarked handmade paper and bound in decorated suede. This edition was finished January 27, 1899 and differs from the 1898 editions in color disbursement. In this edition the large initial letter on the first page of the text is printed in red and filled with hand applied gold. There is a circle and anchor device on page 15 and The Dipsy Chanty at the head of page 9 is printed in red. This edition includes L'Envoi and many of the examined copies are not numbered nor signed and the limiting statement page shows evidence of being tipped in. There were supposedly 80 specially illumined copies though none have been examined.

40. ESSAYS OF ELIA
By Charles Lamb
8½" x 5¾" 175 pages.
Body copy set in Old Style Antique.
970 copies printed in two colors on Kelmscott handmade paper with initial letters hand drawn.100 copies specially illumined with water color sketches.
Both editions bound in suede, numbered and signed in Elbert Hubbard's name. Finished January 27, 1899. The specially illumined edition is bound in a suede cover with a blind stamped design by Denslow. The regular edition is in a plain suede cover.

41. ESSAY ON FRIENDSHIP, THE
By Ralph Waldo Emerson
7¾" x 5½" 53 pages.
Body copy set in Caslon.
925 copies printed on Roycroft handmade paper. Decorations designed by Samuel Warner. 50 copies were supposedly especially illumined by Lawrence

Mazzanovich. 25 copies printed on Japan Vellum. Binding was supposed to be suede but all copies examined have been in variants of paper over boards. Two of the Japan Vellum editions have been bound in three-quarter leather. Many copies of this book were illumined by the staff artists and are signed by them. All copies are numbered and signed in Elbert Hubbard's name.
Completed July 10, 1899. (See *Are They Real?*)

42. FRIENDSHIP'S GARLAND
By William Marion Reedy
8" x 5" 8 pages (self cover).
Body copy set in Old Style Antique.
Reprinted from the St. Louis Mirror of May 4, 1899. Done in two colors on hand made papers. Edition run unknown. The initial letters have the look of Denslow's work.

43. HOUSE OF LIFE, THE
By Dante Gabriel Rossetti
7¾" x 5¾" 114 pages.
Body copy set in Old Style Antique.
925 copies printed in one color on Roycroft hand made paper and bound in 3/4 leather or suede. The edition was illumined, signed and numbered in Elbert Hubbard's name. 25 copies specially illumined by hand and bound in suede. Signed and numbered in Elbert Hubbard's name.There is no difference at all between examined copies of these two editions except for the text of the limiting statement.

44. INTELLECTUAL LIFE, THE
By Philip Gilbert Hamerton
10" x 8" 207 pages.
Body copy set in Old Style Antique.
960 copies printed on Roycroft handmade paper. The initial letters were hand drawn and the edition was numbered and signed in Elbert Hubbard's name. Binding is paper over boards with suede back and corners. Finished October 3, 1899.

The Message to Garcia editions noted below are not the complete listings; that is a task that will never be done since the editions are not all dated I have only noted the points of difference between editions that would facilitate identification.

45. MESSAGE TO GARCIA, A Being a Small Homily
By Elbert Hubbard
7¾" x 5¾" 14 pages.
Body copy set in Caslon.
1,000 copies printed for the New York Central System. First edition carries the New York Central advertisement on the back cover. Cover is printed in red with yellow thread binding.
 a. (another copy)
Notes 920 copies numbered and signed. b. (another copy)

Notes 928 copies numbered and signed. c. (another copy)
Notes 925 copies numbered and signed.
46. MESSAGE TO GARCIA, A
8 ⅟₁₆" x 5⅝" 11 pages.
Bound in brown paper with two point rule boxing type and shield with diagonal and crescent in red. Railroad ad on inside front cover. Title page has decorative border with red fleur-de-lis ornaments in red above and below type.
Statement on next recto states that total of booklets issued to October 1st, 1899 is 981,000. Denslow galleon initial letter on page one with headline in two lines with ornaments. Two color interior printing. Colophon statement in red. Colophon device in red on inside back cover. Back cover has notice on "Message" printing.
a. Brown paper cover with solid six point rule around cover type which is set in a bolder type than above.
b. 7⅞" x 5⅞" 9 pages.
Two point rule border around type. Same bold type as (a) with torch as ornament. Railroad ad on inside front cover. Title page set in different type and different border in one color. Interior printed in one color. Quotation from Proverbs 21:13 opposite from copyright notices. Different Denslow galleon ornamental initial on page one. New interior type composition. New railroad ad on page 12. New colophon device on inside back cover. "Message to Garcia" as on back cover.
c. 7¾" x 5¹³⁄₁₅ 14 pages.
Same cover as (b). Railroad ad is on inside front cover. Different title page type within same border as (b). Proverb missing. One color interior.
d. 7¾" x 5⅞" 9 pages.
Gray cover stock with six point rule boxing bold type in red in upper left and Roycroft device drawn by Bertha Hubbard in red in lower right corner. Inside front cover has ad for House of Life. Title page same as (b). Proverb is opposite copyright page and has leaf ornaments in red top and bottom.
e. 7⅝" x 5⅞" 14 pages.
Bound in dark brown suede. Printed in one color on Japan Vellum with hand illumined title page. Same typographic treatment as (d) but subhead on (d) reads: "Being a Preachment by Elbert Hubbard", while this edition reads: "A Preachment by Elbert Hubbard" . Limited to 925 signed and numbered copies. Has small galleon initial letter on page one.
f. 8⅛" x 5⅛" 11 pages.
Bound in brown paper. Ad on inside front cover notes availability of the Message and the limited edition of 1,000 copies. The title page is typographic without a border and has the Denslow seahorse Roycroft symbol in red. Box with lantern decorations in ad for message is on the back of the title page. Page one has a new decorative initial which is hand colored. The New York Central ad remains on the back cover.
g. 8⅝" x 5¾" 11 pages.
Cover same as (f). Title page has decorated border and Denslow seahorse. 1,000 copies specially illumined, numbered and signed. Page one differs from (f). Here headline is broken into two lines, all caps, with a different set of ornaments used. (f) is set in one line, caps and small caps.

47. MESSAGE TO GARCIA, A
Being a Preachment by Elbert Hubbard
8⅝" x 5⅝" 11 pages.
Body copy set in Old Style Antique.
Printed in two colors on Boxmoor and bound in suede. The title page has the Denslow seahorse Roycroft mark. Limiting statement opposite page one notes hand illumination and limited to 1,000 copies. It is signed and numbered in Elbert Hubbard's name. The only illumination in copies examined is a reuse of the Denslow galleon initial letter to begin the essay.
Other points to examine are the use of green ink in the colophon and the omission of the New York Central statement.

48. PERSIAN PEARL
By Clarence Darrow
8⅝" x 5½" 175 pages.
Body copy set in Old Style Antique.
980 copies printed on Boxmoor in two colors and bound in paper over boards with suede back or in limp suede. Completed April 1,1899. All copies examined are numbered in the limiting statement but not signed.

49. RUBAIYAT OF OMAR KHAYYAM, THE
5¾" x 7⅞" 67 pages.
Body copy set in Caslon.
920 copies numbered and signed by Elbert Hubbard. Printed in three colors, yellow, green and black, on Boxmoor and bound in suede. Cover, title page and colophon device designed by Denslow. The 1901 catalog lists one hand illumined copy printed on Japan Vellum and bound in full levant by Louis Kinder.

50. RUBAIYAT OF OMAR KHAYYAM
5½" x 7" 67 pages.
Body copy set in Caslon.
920 copies printed in one color and bound in suede. This is similar in make up to above except that hand coloring has been used instead of extra press color runs. This edition completed September 10, 1899.

51. RUBAIYAT OF OMAR KHAYYAM
5½" x 7" 67 pages.
Body copy set in Caslon.
Printed in one color on Boxmoor with hand decorations. Using the same interior make-up as previous two entries. However, this is a separate edition with considerable points of difference. It has a title page made up of type and printers decorations rather than the Denslow or Warner title page design used in the other 1899 editions. The limitation statement uses an ampersand at the end of the first line instead of spelling out "and" as above. It lacks a colophon device opposite the colophon statement. The colophon statement ends with the Roycroft/Denslow mark instead of the Bertha Hubbard mark. Finally, and the only point that need be noted in comparison, is that this edition was completed March 10, 1899.

52. SONNETS OF SHAKESPEARE, THE
7¾″ x 5⅝″ 162 pages.
Body copy set in Old Style Antique.
980 copies printed on Roycroft handmade paper and bound in paper over boards with suede spine and corners. One color was used in the body of the book with green and red restricted to the title page, colophon and colophon device. Decorated initial letters were hand colored. The edition was numbered and signed in Elbert Hubbard's name. 12 copies printed on Japan Vellum and bound 3/4 or full levant.

53. TIME AND CHANCE
A Romance and a History; Being the Story of the Life of a Man (John Brown)
By Elbert Hubbard
7¾″ x 5″ 582 pages (two volumes).
Body copy set in Caslon Old Style. Printed in two colors on unmarked laid paper. Photogravure frontispiece of Ruth Crosby (volume one) and John Brown (volume two) on Japan Vellum. Volumes bound in paper over boards with suede spine and corners. Completed August 1, 1899.

1900
54. BOOK OF THE ROYCROFTERS, THE Catalog for 1900
7⅝″ x 6″ 32 pages plus ads.
Body copy set in Bookman. Printed in two colors on Roycroft handmade paper with 16 photogravures of Roycroft workers and shops. Bound in suede. A good reference and source of photos of the personnel of the shop.

55. CATALOGUE AND SOME COMMENTS, A
7¾″ x 6″ 80 pages.
Body copy set in Old Style Antique. Printed on Roycroft handmade paper with 16 photogravures printed on Japan Vellum. Bound in suede.

56. CHICAGO TONGUE
By Fra Elbertus (Elbert Hubbard)
7⅞″ x 5¾″ 25 pages.
Body copy set in Caslon. Printed on Boxmoor paper or Roycroft handmade paper and bound in suede. This essay was later issued in paper covers in diverse sizes and cover designs (See pamphlets).

57. CITY OF TAGASTE, THE
By Elbert Hubbard
10⅛″ x 8″ 21 pages.
Body copy set in Caslon Old Style.
940 copies printed on Roycroft handmade paper and bound in 3/4 suede or decorated suede. 50 copies printed on Imperial Japan Vellum, specially hand illumined and bound 3/4 levant. The illumination is two hand colored borders and one tailpiece designed by Louis Rhead. Edition numbered and signed by

Elbert Hubbard's name. *(See Are They Real? for possible second edition of this entry.)*

58. KING OF THE GOLDEN RIVER, THE
By John Ruskin
7¾" x 5¾" 75 pages.
Body copy set in Caslon Old Style.
General edition printed in two colors, black and orange, on Boxmoor and bound in suede. 350 copies specially illumined in general edition. 40 copies printed on Japan Vellum in suede binding. The volume was designed by Samuel Warner.

59. LAST RIDE, THE
By Robert Browning
7¾" x 5¾" 10 pages.
Body copy set in Monotype 16E.
940 copies printed on Roycroft handmade paper, French folded. Each stanza has specially illumined borders around copy block. The type is printed in blue. Binding is paper over boards with vellum back and corners though some copies were bound in full vellum with cloth ties. 50 copies printed on Japan Vellum and bound in various styles. 25 copies printed on Classic Vellum and bound in hand tooled full levant. Each copy in the several paper and binding variants was numbered and signed in Elbert Hubbard's name.

60. LITTLE JOURNEYS TO THE HOMES OF ENGLISH AUTHORS, VOLUME SIX, NEW SERIES (Book 1)
By Elbert Hubbard
7⅝" x 5¾" 144 pages.
Body and copy set in Old Style Antique.
947 copies printed on Roycroft watermarked handmade paper in two colors and bound in either suede or 3/4 suede. The edition was hand illumined, numbered and signed in Elbert Hubbard's name. Another copy examined has 148 pages. The extra four pages are the Samuel Johnson essay. The identification of volume six on the left and new series on the right top of the title page border are missing in this copy. The limitation statement is identical to the above copy.

61. LITTLE JOURNEYS TO THE HOMES OF ENGLISH AUTHORS, VOLUME SEVEN, NEW SERIES (Book ll)
By Elbert Hubbard
7⅝" x 5¾" 162 pages.
Body copy set in Old Style Antique.
947 copies printed in two colors on Roycroft handmade paper and bound in suede or 3/4 suede. Signed in Elbert Hubbard's name and usually hand illumined. Another copy examined has 161 pages and lacks limitation page. This copy is bound in paper over boards with suede spine.
The first year that the Roycroft Printing Shop produced the Little Journeys. and they produced a limited and a regular edition monthly. The limited edition was printed on Roycroft watermarked handmade paper and the regular edition was done on Boxmoor. Hand illumination, which was really hand coloring/oring of initials and borders ,was part of the limited series and suede was used as the binding . The regular edition was bound in paper.

62. LITTLE JOURNEYS TO THE HOMES OF ENGLISH AUTHORS
By Elbert Hubbard.

William Morris.
925 copies printed on handmade and bound in suede. Numbered and signed in Elbert Hubbard's name.

Robert Browning
925 copies printed on handmade and bound in suede. Numbered and signed in Elbert Hubbard's name. Regular edition as noted above.

Tennyson
925 copies printed on handmade and bound in suede. Numbered and signed in Elbert Hubbard's name. Regular edition as noted above.

Robert Burns
925 copies printed on handmade and bound in suede. Numbered and signed in Elbert Hubbard's name. Regular edition as noted above.

John Milton
925 copies printed on handmade and bound in suede. Numbered and signed in Elbert Hubbard's name. Regular edition as noted above.

Samuel Johnson
925 copies printed on handmade paper and bound in suede. Numbered and signed in Elbert Hubbard's name. Regular edition as noted above.

Macaulay
940 copies printed on handmade paper and bound in suede. Numbered and signed in Elbert Hubbard's name. Regular edition as noted above.

Byron
925 copies printed on handmade and bound in suede. Numbered and signed in Elbert Hubbard's name. Regular edition as noted above.

Addison
940 copies printed on handmade paper and bound in suede. Numbered and signed in Elbert Hubbard's name. Regular edition as noted above.

Southey
940 copies printed on handmade paper and bound in suede. Numbered and signed in Elbert Hubbard's name. Regular edition as noted above.

Coleridge
940 copies printed on handmade paper and bound in suede. Numbered and signed in Elbert Hubbard's name. Regular edition as noted above.

Disraeli
940 copies printed on handmade paper and bound in suede. Numbered and signed in Elbert Hubbard's name.   Regular edition as noted above.

63. MAUDE
8" x 5" 80 pages
Body copy set in ATF Satanick
By Alfred Lord Tennyson
920 copies printed on Whatman, hand illumined and bound in boards.
100 copies specially illumined, printed on Whatman and bound in boards.
40 copies printed on Japan Vellum in variant bindings.Initials, title page and ornaments designed by Samuel Warner. Copies of this work have been found

bound in suede and 3/4 levant. No information on extent of variant bindings is now available.

64. RUBAIYAT OF OMAR KHAYYAM, THE
8⅝" x 5⅝" 51 pages.
1,000 copies printed in four colors on Boxmoor, hand illumined and bound in suede. Numbered and signed in Elbert Hubbard's name. Interesting calligraphic treatment somewhat in the manner of Walter Crane. The lettering is unsigned and no references to authorship have been found, but I would credit it to Samuel Warner. The calligraphy would have been transferred to letter press plates for the run. The hand illumination mentioned in the advertising is just filling in outlines of borders and initial letters. According to Lane there were 49 copies printed on Japan Vellum, specially bound, but we have seen none.

65. WALT WHITMAN
An Essay by Robert Louis Stevenson with an introductory essay by Elbert Hubbard
8½" x 5½" 91 pages.
Body copy set in Caslon.
Title page designed by Louis Rhead. Edition printed on Boxmoor with hand illumined initial letters and bound in suede. 50 copies specially illumined and signed by Roycroft illuminators. Bound in suede.

1901
66. DREAMS By Olive Schreiner
10⅜" x 8⅜" 82 pages.
Body copy set in ATF Satanick.
Regular edition printed in two colors on Roycroft handmade paper and bound in paper over boards with suede spine. 100 copies printed on Imperial Japan Vellum and bound in hand tooled 3/4 leather. Both editions have typography by Andrew Andrews; title page and decoration by Jerome Conner.

67. LITTLE JOURNEYS TO THE HOMES OF GREAT MUSICIANS, VOLUME EIGHT, NEW SERIES (Book 1)
By Elbert Hubbard
7⅝" x 5¾" 158 pages.
Body copy set in Old Style Antique.
947 copies printed in two colors on Roycroft watermarked handmade paper and bound in suede or 3/4 suede. Hand illumined with illuminator's mark on limitation page. Numbered and signed with Elbert Hubbard's name. Another edition, lacking limitation statement page and having 147 numbered pages, is bound in paper over boards, with a suede spine.

68. LITTLE JOURNEYS TO THE HOMES OF GREAT MUSICIANS, VOLUME NINE, NEW SERIES (Book II)
By Elbert Hubbard
7⅝" x 5¾" 149 pages.
Body copy set in Old Style Antique.
940 copies printed in two colors on Roycroft watermarked handmade paper and bound in suede or 3/4 suede. Signed with Elbert Hubbard's name on limitation

page. Hand illumined. Another edition has 137 pages printed in one color and is bound in paper over boards with suede spine.

69. LITTLE JOURNEYS TO THE HOMES OF GREAT MUSICIANS
By Elbert Hubbard
Wagner.
940 copies printed on handmade paper bound in suede. Illumined, numbered and signed in Elbert Hubbard's name. Regular edition printed on handmade paper and bound in paper.
Paganini.
(Same as above)
Chopin.
(Same as above)
Mozart.
(Same as above)
Bach.
(Same as above)
Mendelsohn.
(Same as above).
Liszt
(Same as above)
Beethoven.
(Same as above)
Handel
(Same as above)
Verdi.
(Same as above)
Schumann.
(Same as above)
Brahms.
(Same as above)

70. MESSAGE TO GARCIA AND THIRTEEN OTHER THINGS, A
By Elbert Hubbard
8⅝" x 5½" 166 pages.
Body copy set in Old Style Antique.
Regular edition printed in two colors on Boxmoor and bound in paper over boards with paper labels. 450 copies issued with facsimile manuscript pages inserted. 50 copies printed in two colors on Imperial Japan Vellum and hand illumined. Bound in 3/4 calf or special order leather bindings. Numbered and signed in Elbert Hubbard's name.

71. OLD JOHN BURROUGHS
By Elbert Hubbard
8" x 5" 19 pages.
Body copy set in Caslon. Regular edition printed on Dickinson handmade, with Roycroft watermark. Manuscript reproductions and photo of Burroughs printed on Japan Vellum. Title page, initials and colophon device were hand illumined. Bound in paper over boards with cloth spine. Some copies were bound in 3/4 leather with extra illumination. Number of regular and specially illumined

copies are unknown. There were 12 copies printed on Japan Vellum and bound full levant. I have not seen any of this special edition.

72. POEMS
By Edgar Allen Poe with a foreword by Michael Monahan
9" x 5¾" 54 pages.
Body copy set in Caslon.
Regular edition printed on Kelmscott handmade paper with frontispiece portrait of Poe on vellum. Title page and ornaments designed by Samuel Warner, typography by Andrew Andrews. Bound in suede. 100 copies printed on Imperial Japan Vellum. Binding could be 3/4 leather or boards with suede back strap.

73. STORY OF A PASSION, THE
By Irving Bacheller
7⅞" x 5¾" 14 pages.
Body copy set in Caslon.
Regular edition printed in two colors on Roycroft handmade, with hand illumined title page and running heads. Bound in suede. 50 copies printed on Imperial Japan Vellum; hand illumined and bound in 3/4 leather. Numbered and signed in Elbert Hubbard's name. The Elbert Hubbard Museum has a copy bound in paper over boards with suede spine. There is also a variation in the weight of the paper in the regular edition.

74. WILL O' THE MILL
By Robert Louis Stevenson
7¾" x 5⅞" 53 pages.
Body copy set in Old Style Antique.
Printed in one color on Boxmoor. Portrait, ornaments and initial letters by Samuel Warner. Typography by Andrew Andrews. Regular edition bound in suede.100 copies printed on Imperial Japan Vellum and bound in 3/4 leather. 350 copies were specially illumined. Numbered and signed in Elbert Hubbard's name. Special illumination was just coloring of printed initial letters.

1902
75. CHRISTMAS CAROL, A
By Charles Dickens
8½" x 5½" 141 pages.
Body copy set in Caslon.
Regular edition printed in two colors on Boxmoor. Bound in suede. 100 copies printed on Japan Vellum.Title page, headbands and tailpiece designed by Samuel Warner. Composition by Charles Rosen and presswork by Otto Franz. Variations in binding include 3/4 leather, full vellum with cloth ties and paper over boards with suede spine and corners.

76. CONTEMPLATIONS
Being Several Short Essays, Helpful Sermonettes, Epigrams and Orphic Sayings from the Writings of Elbert Hubbard
11" x 8¾" 120 pages.

Body copy set in McFarland Series.
Regular edition printed on Boxmoor and bound in paper over boards with
suede back strap and corners. 100 copies printed on Imperial Japan Vellum and
bound in 3/4 leather. Also available in modeled leather. Ornaments were
designed by Richard Kruger, press work by Otto Franz and composition by
Charles Rosen.

77. HAMLET
By William Shakespeare
10" x 8" 172 pages.
Body copy set in Bruce Roman.
Regular edition printed in one color on Roycroft watermarked handmade paper
and bound in paper over boards with suede back. Some of this edition have
illumined title pages and suede corners as well as suede back. An edition of 100
copies was printed on Imperial; hand illumined and bound in three quaarter
levant.

78. LITTLE JOURNEYS TO THE HOMES OF EMINENT ARTISTS, VOL-UME TEN (Book 1)
By Elbert Hubbard
7⅝" x 5¾" 165 pages.
Body copy set in Old Style Antique.
940 copies printed in two colors on Roycroft watermarked handmade paper and
bound in suede or 3/4 suede. Hand illumined and signed in Elbert Hubbard's
name.

79. LITTLE JOURNEYS TO THE HOMES OF EMINENT ARTISTS, VOL-UME ELEVEN (Book ll)
By Elbert Hubbard
7⅝" x 5¾" 158 pages.
Body copy set in Old Style Antique.
Printed in two colors on Roycroft watermarked handmade paper and bound in
suede or 3/4 suede. Hand illumined, but the limitation statement and illuminator's signature are lacking.

80. LITTLE JOURNEYS TO THE HOMES OF EMINENT ARTISTS
By Elbert Hubbard
Raphael
940 copies printed on handmade paper and bound in suede. Illumined, num-
bered and signed in Elbert Hubbard's name. Regular edition printed on hand-
made paper and bound in paper.
Leonardo.
(Same as above.)
Botticelli.
(Same as above)
Thorwaldsen.
(Same as above)
Gainsborough.
(Same as above)

Velasquez
(Same as above)
Corot
(Same as above)
Correggio.
(Same as above)
Edwin Abbey.
(Same as above)
Bellini.
(Same as above)
Cellini.
(Same as above)

81. LODGING FOR THE NIGHT, A
By Robert Louis Stevenson
7⅞" X 5" 44 pages.
Body copy set in Bruce Roman. Printed in one color on Roycroft handmade
paper. Photogravure portrait of Stevenson on Japan Vellum. Bound in suede.
100 copies printed on Japan Vellum, hand illumined and bound 3/4 leather.
Some copies of this edition were also bound in full levant. Finished October 16,
1902.

82. SELF RELIANCE
By Ralph Waldo Emerson
7½"x 5¼" 46 pages.
Body copy set in Bruce Roman. Printed in one color on Roycroft watermarked
laid paper. Bound in suede. 100 copies printed on Japan Vellum and bound 3/4
leather. Both editions have frontispiece photogravure of Emerson. Completed
July 28, 1902.

1903
83. AS YOU LIKE IT
By William Shakespeare
10" X 7¾" 122 pages.
Body copy set in Bruce Roman. Regular edition printed in one color on Roycroft
paper and bound in paper over boards with suede back strap or "Alicia". An
edition of 100 copies was printed on Imperial Japan Vellum, specially illumined
and bound in tooled 3/4 leather. Borders and heads designed by Samuel
Warner; press work by Otto Franz.

84. BOOK OF SONGS, THE
By Heinrich Heine
7⅝" X 5¾" 116 pages.
Body copy set in Old Style Antique. Printed in two colors on Boxmoor and
bound in suede. 100 copies printed on Japan Vellum and bound in 3/4 German
marbled calf.

85. CRY OF THE LITTLE PEOPLES, THE
By Richard LeGallienne
5¾" x 4" 5 pages.
Body copy set in Monotype No. 1A
Bound in decorated paper printed in three colors with shamrocks in green as main decoration. Text is printed on Roycroft handmade paper in one color with hand illumined decorative initials. Press run unknown. This is the first separate printing of LeGallienne's poem.

86. FANTASMA
By Arcadius Yonge
7½" x 5½" 152 pages.
Body copy set in Satanick.
Printed in one color on Roycroft handmade paper in an edition of 250 copies and in edition of fifty copies on Japan Vellum. Both editions bound in suede.

87. FRIENDSHIP
By Henry David Thoreau
11½" x 7¾" 36 pages.
Body copy set in Cheltenham.
Printed on Roycroft handmade paper with hand drawn initial letters and hand colored colophon device. Bound in paper over boards with suede spine. This is noted in the 1905/06 catalog as "a few copies", but it is obviously a separate edition, and, in my opinion, one of the handsomest books of the press.

88. FRIENDSHIP
By Henry David Thoreau
7½" x 5½" 45 pages.
Body copy set in Cheltenham.
Regular edition printed on Boxmoor with three color title page. Bound in suede or paper over boards with cloth spine.50 copies printed on Japan Vellum with hand drawn initials. Bound in 3/4 leather.10 copies printed on Classic Vellum with hand drawn initials and 40 free hand drawings. Bound in full levant.

89. GRAY'S ELEGY
By Thomas Gray
7¾" x 5¾" 16 pages.
Body copy set in Caslon. Regular edition printed in two colors, blue and beige, on Boxmoor French folded. A "few" copies were advertised printed on Japan Vellum and bound 3/4 leather. None of this edition have been found. This book, except for the solid colored title page, uses the same borders as Browning's Last Ride (1900).

90. HOLLY TREE, THE
By Charles Dickens
8½" x 5⅝" 66 pages.
Regular edition printed on Boxmoor and bound in suede. Borders designed by Samuel Warner, typography by Newell White and presswork by George Parker. A "few" (none examined) on Japan Vellum and bound in tooled 3/4 leather.

91. LITTLE JOURNEYS TO THE HOMES OF EMINENT ORATORS, VOL-UME TWELVE (Book 1)
By Elbert Hubbard
7⅝"x 5¼" 182 pages.
Body copy set in Old Style Antique.
Printed in two colors on Roycroft watermarked handmade paper and bound in 3/4 suede. No limitation page in this volume. Illumination is spotty, and the entire volume is less decorative than its predecessors.

92. LITTLE JOURNEYS TO THE HOMES OF EMINENT ORATORS, VOL-UME THIRTEEN (Book II)
By Elbert Hubbard
7⅝" x 5¾" 184 pages.
Body copy set in Old Style Antique.
Printed in one color on Roycroft watermarked handmade paper and bound in 3/4 suede. No limitation page as above.

93. LITTLE JOURNEYS TO THE HOMES OF EMINENT ORATORS
By Elbert Hubbard
Pericles.
We cannot determine if there was a limited, illumined edition of this essay. No advertising or copies examined have resolved this question. Printed on hand-made paper and suede bound. Also bound in paper and boards.
Mark Anthony.
Same as above.
Savanarola
Same as above.
Martin Luther.
Same as above.
Edmund Burke.
Same as above.
William Pitt.
Same as above.
Marat.
Same as above.
Robert Ingersoll
Same as above.
John Randolph.
Same as above.
Thomas Starr King
Same as above.
Henry Ward Beecher.
Same as above.
Wendell Phillips.
Same as above.

94. LITTLE JOURNEY TO THE HOME OF JOAQUIN MILLER
By Elbert Hubbard. Also a Study of the Man and his Work by George Wharton James

7¾" x5⅝" 106 pages.
Body copy set in Cheltenham.
Regular edition printed in two colors on Boxmoor and bound in suede.
100 copies printed on Japan Vellum and bound in 3/4 levant. Numbered and signed in Elbert Hubbard's name.

95. MESSAGE TO GARCIA, A
Being a Preachment by Elbert Hubbard
7"x 5⅜" 10 pages.
Body copy set in Monotype 68J
100 copies printed on Japan Vellum and bound in full levant with Jansenite inner cover. Title page, initial letters and colophon device hand illumined. Photo of Rowan, George Daniels and Elbert Hubbard mounted on coarse brown paper. Edition signed on bottom of front flyleaf by Rowan and with Hubbard's name. (See Message to Garcia) for the background story of this edition).

96. VIRGINIBUS PUERISQUE
By Robert Louis Stevenson
7⅞" x 5¼" 77 pages.
Body copy set in Elzevir.
Printed in one color on Roycroft handmade paper and bound in suede. 100 copies printed on Japan Vellum and offered in 3/4 levant binding. Some of the regular and limited edition were hand illumined. There is also a variant parchment binding and a handsome incised leather binding in the regular edition.

1904
97. BOY FROM MISSOURI VALLEY, THE
By Elbert Hubbard
7¾" x 5¼" 12 pages.
Body copy set in Cheltenham. Printed on Boxmoor, paper bound.

98. COMPENSATION
By Ralph Waldo Emerson
7½" x 5¾" 44 pages.
Body copy set in Condensed Roman.
Printed in two colors on Boxmoor with a photogravure of the "Old Manse" on Japan Vellum as frontispiece. Bound in suede.100 copies printed on Japan Vellum and bound in 3/4 leather.

99. CONSECRATED LIVES
By Elbert Hubbard
8½" x 6¾" 101 pages.
Body copy set in McFarland Series, Inland Type Foundry.
Printed in two colors on Dickinson paper with sepia photogravure of Roycroft chapel and title page on cream unmarked stock. Bound in suede, boards or 3/4 leather. 100 copies printed on Japan Vellum and bound in 3/4 levant. Numbered and signed in Elbert Hubbard's name.

100. KING LEAR
By William Shakespeare
10¼" x 8" 147 pages.
Body copy set in Scotch Roman. Regular edition on Roycroft handmade paper; bound in paper over boards with suede backstrap. 100 copies on Japan Vellum and bound in 3/4 leather. Specially illumined, signed and numbered in Elbert Hubbard's name.

101. KING LEAR
By William Shakespeare
10¼" x 8" 147 pages.
Body copy set in Scotch Roman.
18 copies printed on kraft paper and bound in paper over boards with suede backstop. Cover done in crude hand lettering and reads: "King Lear - As Written by W. Shakespeare and Done into a Book by Ye Merrie Roycrofters for Ye Dramatic Club". Colophon done in the same manner. Contents identical to regular edition. This was obviously done for fun and distributed among the Roycrofters and close friends.

102. LITTLE JOURNEYS TO THE HOMES OF GREAT PHILOSOPHERS, VOLUME FOURTEEN (Book 1)
By Elbert Hubbard
7⅝"x 5¾" 176 pages.
Body copy set in Old Style Antique.
Printed in one color on Roycroft watermarked handmade paper and bound in 3/4 suede. No limitation statement.

103. LITTLE JOURNEYS TO THE HOMES OF GREAT PHILOSOPHERS, VOLUME FIFTEEN (Book ll)
By Elbert Hubbard
7⅝" x 5¾" 189 pages.
Body copy set in Old Style Antique.
Printed in one color on Roycroft watermarked handmade paper and bound in 3/4 suede. No limitation statement and some spotty illumination.

104. LITTLE JOURNEYS TO THE HOMES OF GREAT PHILOSOPHERS
By Elbert Hubbard
Socrates.
Printed in one color on Roycroft handmade paper and bound in paper or boards.
Seneca.
(Same as above)
Aristotle.
(Same as above)
Marcus Aurelius.
(Same as above)
Spinoza.
(Same as above)

Swedenborg
(Same as above)
Immanuel Kant.
(Same as above)
Auguste Comte. .
(Same as above)
Voltaire.
(Same as above)
Herbert Spencer.
(Same as above)
Schopenhauer.
(Same as above)
Henry D. Thoreau.
(Same as above)

105. LORD'S PRAYER, THE
By Clara Kinne Whealen
5⅝" x 4¼" 11 pages.
Body copy set in Cheltenham and Satanick. Printed on handmade paper with hand illumined initial letters. (Another vanity production; Mrs. Whealen did not compose the subject matter).

106. MAN OF SORROWS, THE A Little Journey to the Home of Jesus of Nazareth
By Elbert Hubbard
7¾" x 5¾" 150 pages.
Body copy set in Scotch Roman.
Printed in one color on Roycroft handmade paper. Decorated title page, borders and initials in outline. Bound in suede. There are variants in the suede bindings design. 90 copies printed on Japan Vellum; bound in three quarter leather. Another editions of 102 copies on Japan Vellum, hand illumined and bound in three quarter levant has been reported. 10 copies were bound in hand tooled full leather. It is odd that no copy of this book has been found with hand illumination since the printed decorative elements are obviously designed for hand embellishment.

107. RUBAIYAT OF OMAR KHAYYAM, THE
Done into English by Edward FitzGerald with an Introduction by Clarence S. Darrow
4⅞" x 7⅛" 40 pages for Darrow essay; 51 pages for Rubaiyat.
Body copy set in Scotch Roman.
This edition has two verses by Charles P. Nettelson after the title page followed by "The Persian Pearl" by Darrow. Printed in two colors, red for Lombardic initials and black for text, on Boxmoor. Bound in suede. 100 copies printed on Japan Vellum and offered in various binding styles.

108. SONG OF MYSELF
By Walt Whitman
8½" x 6½" 70 pages.

Body copy set in McFarland.
Printed in two colors on Dickinson handmade paper and bound in suede.
100 copies printed on Japan Vellum and bound 3/4 leather. Of the regular edition, copies have been examined that were printed on Whatman and bound in Modeled Leather. There is insufficient evidence to determine if this could be a separate edition. Also some copies of both editions have hand colored title pages.

1905
109. BALLAD OF READING GAOL, THE
By Oscar Wilde
7½" x 5¾" 57 pages.
Body copy set in Cheltenham.
Regular edition printed on machine made paper in two colors with hand applied gold outline to initial letters. Bound in suede. 100 copies printed on Japan Vellum and bound 3/4 leather. Some of the regular edition were available in modeled leather binding.

110. BOOK OF DAYS, A
By F. Sydnor Cartmell
8¼" x 5¼" 26 pages.
Body copy set in Satanick.
Printed on Roycroft handmade paper and bound in paper over boards. Press run unknown.

111. ELBERT HUBBARD, A LITTLE JOURNEY TO THE HOME OF
By Terence V. Powderly
7⅝" x 5¾" 15 pages.
Body copy set in Old Style Antique.
Done in the standard Little Journey format.

112. ESSAY ON NATURE, THE
By Ralph Waldo Emerson
7⅞" x 5" 91 pages.
Body copy set in Old Style Antique.
Printed in two colors on Dickinson with Dard Hunter title page, initials tails and colophon device. Bound in blind stamped suede in a Dard Hunter design. There is a variant cover design in the suede and 50 copies were advertised as being bound "Repousse". 100 copies printed on Imperial Japan Vellum and bound in three-quarter levant. Most were hand illumined. Pagination of foreword matter changed in this limited edition.

113. ESSAY ON SELF-RELIANCE, THE
By Ralph Waldo Emerson
8" x 5⅛" 51 pages.
Body copy set in Bruce Roman.
Printed on Roycroft handmade paper in two colors, black and green, with the green being restricted to the title page and colophon device. Bound in limp

suede. 100 copies printed on Japan Vellum and bound 3/4 leather. Both editions illustrated with frontispiece portrait of Emerson by Schnieder. We have examined two unlimited copies printed on Japan Vellum one bound in 3/4 leather and the other in suede. We cannot determine if this is another unnumbered edition or copies made up on Japan Vellum the type forms of the regular edition.

114. ESSAY SILENCE, THE
By Elbert Hubbard
5¼" x 3½"
One of Elbert Hubbard's best put-ons. The book is blank pages and was sold for thirty cents in stamps. Usually bound in suede, it was made up of paper trimmings and was a constant offering of the press after 1905.

115. FORMULA FOR BOOKBINDERS
By Louis H. Kinder
11½" x 8¾" 115 pages.
Body copy set in Scotch Roman. 490 copies printed on Imperial Japan Vellum in two colors. Bound in paper over boards with cloth spine. Some copies bound in 3/4 levant. Photo illustrations of Mr. Kinder's work are used.

116. LAW OF LOVE, THE
By William Marion Reedy
7⅝" x 5¾" 159 pages.
Body copy set in Cheltenham Bold.
Regular edition printed on Boxmoor in three colors and bound in suede.
50 copies of regular edition bound in modeled calf. 50 copies on Japan Vellum bound in marbled paper over boards with suede back. 106 copies printed on Japan Vellum and bound in 3/4 leather. 2 copies examined bound in full leather.

117. LITTLE JOURNEYS TO THE HOMES OF GREAT SCIENTISTS, VOLUME SIXTEEN (Book 1)
By Elbert Hubbard
7⅝" x 5¾" 189 pages.
Body copy set in Old Style Antique. Printed in one color on Roycroft watermarked handmade paper and bound in 3/4 suede. No limitation statement.

118. LITTLE JOURNEYS TO THE HOMES OF GREAT SCIENTISTS, VOLUME SEVENTEEN (Book ll)
By Elbert Hubbard
7⅝" x 5¾" 151 pages.
Body copy set in Old Style Antique. Printed in one color on Roycroft watermarked handmade paper and bound in 3/4 suede. No limitation statement.

119. LITTLE JOURNEYS TO THE HOMES OF GREAT SCIENTISTS
By Elbert Hubbard
Copernicus.
Printed in one color on Roycroft handmade paper and bound in paper or boards.
Galileo.

(Same as above)
Sir Isaac Newton.
(Same as above)
Humboldt.
(Same as above)
Herschel .
(Same as above)
Charles Darwin.
(Same as above)
Ernest Haeckel.
(Same as above)
Carl Von Linnaeus.
(Same as above)
Thomas Huxley.
(Same as above)
John Tyndall .
(Same as above)
Alfred Russel Wallace.
(Same as above)
John Fiske.
(Same as above)

120. MAN OF SORROWS, THE
By Elbert Hubbard
8" x 5" 111 pages.
Body copy set in Scotch Roman.
Printed in one color on Ruisdael with a Dard Hunter title page on Japan Vellum
tipped in. Title page is hand illumined. Bound in suede with a Dard Hunter
cover design.

121. MAN OF SORROWS, THE
By Elbert Hubbard
8" x 5" 111 pages.
Body copy set in Scotch Roman.
100 copies printed in one color on Imperial Japan Vellum with hand decorated
title page, initial letters and colophon device. Bound in 3/4 or full levant.
The interior make up of this book is identical to previous entry printed on
Ruisdael, but the title page and arrangement of foreword matter are different so
we are recording this as a separate edition. The title pages of this edition show
considerable hand work and should not be used as identifying points.

122. PHILISTINE INDEX AND CONCORDANCE
Compiled by Julia Ditto Young for volumes I through XX
282 pages printed and bound to match the Philistine bound volumes. Colophon
statement notes that Mrs. Young began her work on December 1st, 1901, finished
June 3rd, 1903, revised in April 1905 and printed. It also lists the Roycroft Press
publications to that date.

123. RECESSIONAL/BALLAD OF THE EAST AND WEST/L'ENVOI
By Rudyard Kipling
8" x 5" 19 pages.
Printed on Roycroft handmade paper in one color, black, and bound in paper over boards with cloth spine. Press run unknown; this was a private printing for Bertha Herrington.

124. RESPECTABILITY/ITS RISE AND REMEDY
By Fra Elbertus (Elbert Hubbard)
7¾" x 5⅞" 122 pages.
Body copy set in Bookman. Regular edition printed in two colors, brown and black, on Ruisdael and bound in suede. 107 copies printed on Japan Vellum and bound in 3/4 levant. 2 copies bound in hand tooled full levant and cased in hand carved mahogany boxes trimmed with copper.

125. RIP VAN WINKLE
By Washington Irving with a foreword by Joseph Jefferson
7⅞" x 4⅝" 48 pages.
Body copy set in Old Style Antique. Regular edition printed in three colors on Holland handmade paper with Roycroft watermark. Title page and initials designed by Dard Hunter. Bound in suede or paper over boards with suede spine. 100 copies printed on Imperial Japan Vellum and bound 3/4 leather. 50 copies bound in modeled calf.

1906
126. AFTER THE CLOCK STRIKES SIX
by Leo G. Benedict
(Need specs here)
50 copies printed on Italian hand-made paper and bound in full suede.

127. CRIMES AGAINST CRIMINALS
By Robert Ingersoll
7⅞" x 5¾" 59 pages.
Body copy set in Scotch Roman.
Regular edition printed in one color on Roycroft watermarked laid paper and bound in suede. Etchings by Schnieder on Japan Vellum are placed between pages 16 and 17. Another copy bound in suede with variant cover design and second etching between pages 32 and 33. Another copy has frontispiece portrait on vellum by Schnieder and lacks the two inserted plates. No variance in binding. Another copy bound in paper over boards with leather spine. It has a hand colored title page and colophon device. This issue is printed on Roycroft Fabriano handmade and the second illustration is placed between pages 24 and 25. There is an edition limited to 174 copies printed on Imperial Japan Vellum and signed by Elbert Hubbard ll. This edition lacks the two illustrations and is bound in 1/2 leather or 3/4 levant. Two copies are known to be bound in full levant by Kinder.

128. DOG OF FLANDERS, A
By Ouida
8" x 5¾" 90 pages.
Body copy set in Scotch Roman.
Printed in two colors, black and orange, on Roycroft handmade paper. Bound in suede or paper boards with 1/4 suede spine. 110 copies printed on Japan Vellum and bound in suede or paper boards. Numbered and signed in Elbert Hubbard's name.

129. JUNGLE BOOK, THE - A CRITICISM
By Elbert Hubbard
5¾"x 4½" 32 pages.

130. JUSTINIAN AND THEODORA
By Elbert and Alice Hubbard
8" x 5½" 107 pages.
Body copy set in Caslon.
Printed in two colors, black and orange, on Roycroft handmade paper. Title page, running heads, initial letters and colophon device designed by Dard Hunter. Available bound in suede, paper boards, Alicia, 3/4 leather and full tooled levant. Double portraits of Alice and Elbert Hubbard by Schnieder in sepia on vellum as frontispiece. 106 copies printed on Japan Vellum and bound in tooled 3/4 leather. Numbered and signed in Elbert Hubbard's name.

131. LITTLE JOURNEYS TO THE HOMES OF GREAT LOVERS, VOLUME EIGHTEEN (Book 1)
By Elbert Hubbard
7⅝" x 5¾" 164 pages.
Body copy set in Old Style Antique.
Printed in one color on Roycroft watermarked handmade paper. Title page designed by Raymond Nott. Usual binding variations.

132. LITTLE JOURNEYS TO THE HOMES OF GREAT LOVERS, VOLUME NINETEEN (Book II)
By Elbert Hubbard
7⅝" x 5¾" 193 pages.
Body copy set in Old Style Antique.
Printed in one color on Roycroft watermarked handmade paper. Designed by Raymond Nott.

133. LITTLE JOURNEYS TO THE HOMES OF GREAT LOVERS
By Elbert Hubbard
Josiah and Sarah Wedgwood
Printed in one color on Roycroft handmade paper and bound in paper or boards.
William Godwin and Mary .
(Same as above)
Dante and Beatrice.
(Same as above)

John Stuart Mill and Harriet Taylor.
(Same as above)
Parnell and Kitty O'Shea.
(Same as above)
Petrarch and Laura.
(Same as above)
Dante Gabriel Rosetti and Elizabeth Eleanor SiddaL
(Same as above)
Balzac and Madame Hanska.
(Same as above)
Fenelon and Madame Guyon.
(Same as above)
Ferdinand Lassalle and Helene Von Donniges.
(Same as above)
Lord Nelson and Lady Hamilton.
(Same as above)
Robert Louis Stevenson and Fanny Osbourne.
(Same as above)

134. LOVE LIFE & WORK
By Elbert Hubbard
7 x4 ½" 150 pages
Printed in two colors, red and orange, on unmarked laid paper. Decorated title page and initial letters are the work of Dard Hunter though they are unsigned. Bound in blind stamped suede. 90 copies printed on Japan Vellum and bound in 3/4 leather. 2 copies printed on Japan Vellum and bound in full leather. Some copies were bound in modeled leather or paper over boards with suede spine.

135. MAN OF SORROWS, THE
By Elbert Hubbard
8" x 5" 120 pages.
Body copy set in Scotch Roman.
Printed in two colors, brown and black, for title page, just black for text. Done on Roycroft handmade paper and bound in suede. 200 copies printed on Imperial Japan Vellum and bound in 3/4 levant. Numbered and signed in Elbert Hubbard's name.This edition differs from the previous edition in title page and initial/ letter design.

136. MESSAGE TO GARCIA, A Being a Preachment
by Elbert Hubbard
5¹¹⁄₁₆" x 4¼" 30 pages.
Body copy set in Bookman. Printed in two colors on Japan Vellum. Hand colored ornaments and initials.This is the English to Japanese to English edition. Bound in suede.

137. PARADISE - A PROSE IDYLL
By John Sampson Handley
7⅜" x 5½" 23 pages.

Body copy set in Scotch Roman. Printed in two colors on Japan Vellum and bound in paper boards with leather spine. Published by Dodge Publishing and unsigned as a Roycroft production.

138. RECOLLECTIONS
By Dorothy Whitney
8" x 4⅝" 15 pages.
Body copy set in Old Style Antique. Printed in two colors and bound in paper over boards with vellum spine.

139. RUBAIYAT OF OMAR KHAYYAM, THE
With a two stanza introduction by Charles P. Nettleton and a reprint of an address by the Hon. John Hay delivered at the Dinner of the Omar Khayyam Club, London, December 8, 1897
7" x 6" 76 pages.
Body copy set in Cheltenham. Regular edition in seven colors on Ruisdael; bound in suede. Initial letters and title page designed by W. W. Denslow. 103 copies printed on Imperial Japan Vellum and bound in either 3/4 or full leather. Numbered and signed in Elbert Hubbard's name.

140. RUBAIYAT OF OMAR KHAYYAM, THE
6¾" x 5¾" 75 pages.
Body copy set in Cheltenham. Regular edition printed in four colors with Denslow title page and illustrations. Bound in suede. 103 copies printed on Imperial Japan Vellum, numbered and signed Elbert Hubbard. At least one copy bound in full levant.

141. SHREDS AND PATCHES OF VIRGINIA HISTORY
By Mildred Beatty Pierce
7¾" x 5¾" 110 pages.
Body copy set in Caslon. Printed on Roycroft watermarked laid paper. Illustrated with photographs. Bound in paper boards with suede spine or full suede.

142. THOMAS JEFFERSON, A LITTLE JOURNEY AND AN ADDRESS
By Elbert Hubbard and John J. Lentz
8" x 4½" 105 pages.
Body copy set in Scotch Roman.
Printed in two colors on Roycroft watermarked handmade paper with frontispiece portrait on Japan Vellum by Schnieder. Bound in suede. 50 copies printed on Japan Vellum in 3/4 leather.

143. SELF RELIANCE
By Ralph Waldo Emerson
8" x 5⅛" 51 pages.
Body copy set in Bruce Roman.
Printed in two colors with the second color, green, restricted to the title page, decorated border and Roycroft mark at colophon. Text printed in black on Roycroft handmade paper. Regular edition bound in suede. 100 copies printed

on Imperial Japan Vellum and bound in 3/4 levant. Numbered and signed in Elbert Hubbard's name. Both editions illustrated with frontispiece rendering of Emerson by Schnieder.

1907
144. BATTLE OF WATERLOO, THE
By Victor Hugo
7" x 4⅝" 106 pages.
Body copy set in Caslon bold.
Regular edition printed on machine made paper with Roycroft watermark. Title page and initial letters designed by Dard Hunter. Frontispiece portrait by Schnieder. Bound in either suede or paper boards. 194 copies printed on Imperial Japan Vellum and bound 3/4 leather. Numbered and signed in Elbert Hubbard's name.

145. BOOK OF THE ROYCROFTERS, THE
9" x 7" 17 pages.
Body copy set in Cheltenham.
Cover, title page, initial letters, tails and colophon device designed by Dard Hunter. Body copy is printed in black, decorations run in pink, green and black. Photo illustrated. Printed on Boxmoor and bound in paper boards with cloth spine.

146. LIFE AND DEATH
By W. C. Brann
7¾" x 5½" 11 pages.
Hand illumined title page with decorated initials. Bound in suede.

147. LITTLE JOURNEYS TO THE HOMES OF GREAT REFORMERS, VOLUME TWENTY (Book 1)
By Elbert Hubbard
7⅝" x 5¾" 190 pages.
Body copy set in Old Style Antique.
Printed in two colors on Roycroft watermarked handmade paper. Bound in suede, 3/4 suede or 3/4 suede.

148. LITTLE JOURNEYS TO THE HOMES OF GREAT REFORMERS, VOLUME TWENTY-ONE (Book ll)
By Elbert Hubbard
7⅝" x 5¾" 169 pages. Body copy set in Old Style Antique.
Printed in two colors on Roycroft watermarked handmade paper.

149. LITTLE JOURNEYS TO THE HOMES OF GREAT REFORMERS
By Elbert Hubbard
John Wesley.
Printed in two colors on Roycroft handmade paper and bound in paper or boards.
Henry George.
(Same as above)

Garibaldi
(Same as above)
Richard Cobden.
(Same as above)
Thomas Paine.
(Same as above)
John Knox.
(Same as above)
John Bright.
(Same as above)
John Bradlaugh.
(Same as above)
Theodore Parker.
(Same as above)
Oliver Cromwell .
(Same as above)
Anne Hutchinson.
(Same as above)
Jean Jacque s Rousseau.
(Same as above)

150. NEW LEAF, THE
By Ruth Louise Sheldon
Eight page booklet printed in two colors and paper bound.

151. TRIBUTE OF LOVE, A
By C. A. Woolson
7¾" x 5¾" 1O pages.
Body copy set in Caslon.
Two color title page, photo illustrated and bound in suede. One of the many private printings done by the press.

152. VERSES
By "Our Emma"
5⅝" x 3¾" 30 pages.
Body copy set in Caslon. Printed in two colors and bound in suede.

153. WHAT SOME OF THE MULDOON GRADUATES HAVE TO SAY ABOUT THE HYGIENIC INSTITUTE
Two color 47 page promotion for this commercial institution. Suede bound.
Material such as this commercial piece began to appear as Roycroft book offerings. Later they would be available as pamphlets done as sales literature for the clients.

154. WHITE HYACINTHS
By Elbert Hubbard
7" x 4 ⅝" 161 pages.
Body copy set in Caslon.
Printed in three colors on Roycroft watermarked machine made paper. Cover design, title page, initial letters and decorations designed by Dard Hunter.

Photogravure portraits of Alice and Elbert Hubbard on vellum as frontispiece.
Available bound in suede, boards, Alicia, three quarter leather, full tooled
leather and modeled leather.
 a. Variant edition
Same format as above but this edition has 108 pages. The difference is the omis-
sion of the essay In Re Success. It is a true variant and not a collating error since
the typographical treatment of the last sentences of the two editions are differ-
ent. In this edition we have "Mind alone is immortal - Thought is the thing."
The 161 page edition reads "Mind alone is immortal - Thought is THE THING."
There is an edition of 207 copies of the 161 page edition printed on Japan
Vellum and bound in either 3/4 or full leather. It is numbered and signed in
Elbert Hubbard's name.

155. WILLIAM MORRIS BOOK
A Little Journey by Elbert Hubbard and some letters written by Morris to
Robert Thomson
8" x 5¼" 67 pages.
Body copy set in Caslon.
Printed in two colors, red and black, on Roycroft watermarked laid paper.
Photogravure of bas relief of Morris by Jerome Conner and a two page copy of
one of the Morris letters illustrate the book. Bindings were suede, boards, and
Alicia. Special bindings in 3/4 and full levant were offered later. 203 copies
printed on Japan Vellum, numbered and signed in Elbert Hubbard's name were
issued bound in 3/4 levant.

156. WORLD OF JUST YOU AND I, THE
Printed for J. E. Busch
7¾" x 5½" 7 pages.
Body copy set in Cheltenham.
Interesting only for the decorated title page. Suede bound.

1908
157. BIBLIOMANIAC, THE
By John N. W. Pratt
5⅞" x 4⅜" 4 pages.
Body copy set in Monotype 117 J.
Printed in one color on Roycroft handmade and bound in suede. Limiting state-
ment read: "Of this edition only two copies were printed of which this is no.
Another small vanity job by the Roycrofters.

158. BRONCO BOOK, THE
By Captain Jack Crawford
6⅞" x 4½" 143 pages.
Body copy set in Cushing.
Printed in two colors on unmarked laid paper and bound in paper boards with
suede spine or in suede. Frontispiece rendering of Crawford on Japan Vellum by
Gaspard.

159. COMPLETE WRITINGS OF ELBERT HUBBARD, THE
Volume One
11½" x 7¾" 282 pages.
Body copy set in Cheltenham.
Printed in three colors on Roycroft handmade paper. Title page and initial letters by Dard Hunter. The regular edition was limited to 1,000 sets. 15 sets were printed on Japan Vellum and bound in full or 3/4 leather. Volume two, 314 pages; Volume three, 320 pages; Volume four, 364 pages. This is a scarce set and is the best of the Roycroft serial printings The regular edition volumes were issued boxed and unfortunately the books are not matched in leather color, which ranges from brown to green.

160. ESSAY ON SELF-RELIANCE, THE
By Ralph Waldo Emerson
8⅞" x 7" 59 pages.
Body copy set in Cheltenham.
Printed on Roycroft handmade paper in two colors with two color gravure sketch by Schnieder tipped in. Bound in paper boards with cloth spine.
No information on press run or design supervision. The copy in the Elbert Hubbard Museum has a completely different style and placement of cover typography than the copy in the author's collection. The interior makeup of the volume is identical. Copies may be found with a glassine dust cover or printed brown wrapper. This is the first use of a dust cover for a Roycroft publication.

161. HEALTH AND WEALTH
By Elbert Hubbard
7" x 4⅜" 162 pages.
Body copy set in Scotch Roman.
Printed in black and red on heavy laid paper. Photos of Elbert and Alice Hubbard tipped on blue stock sewn into signatures. Bound in decorated suede designed by Dard Hunter, paper boards with suede spine, Alicia, V4 levant and full decorated levant. An unnumbered edition was printed on Japan Vellum and bound in modeled leather.

162. JEFFERSON DAVIS-A JUDICIAL ESTIMATE
By Bishop Charles B. Galloway
7¾" x 5¼" 48 pages.
Body copy printed in Caslon.
Printed in one color and bound in suede. Photo illustrations of Davis and Bishop Galloway.

163. LITTLE JOURNEYS TO THE HOMES OF FAMOUS WOMEN
By Elbert Hubbard
11½" x 7¾" 313 pages.
Body copy set in Cheltenham.
Printed on Boxmoor in three colors with initial letters by Dard Hunter.
Illustrations of Elbert Hubbard and subjects by Mazzanovich and Gaspard.
Bound in paper boards with suede spine. Subjects of this edition were Elizabeth Barrett Browning, Madame Guyon, Harriet Martineau, Charlotte Bronte,

Christina Rossetti, Rosa Bonheur, Madame De Stael, Elizabeth Fry, Mary Lamb, Jane Austen, Empress Josephine, Mary Wollstonecraft Shelly.

164. LITTLE JOURNEYS TO THE HOMES OF GREAT TEACHERS, VOL-UME TWENTY-TWO (Book 1)
By Elbert Hubbard
7⅝" x 5¾" 152 pages.
Body copy set in Old Style Antique.
Printed in two colors on Roycroft watermarked handmade paper with title page, initials, head and tail pieces designed by Dard Hunter.

165. LITTLE JOURNEYS TO THE HOMES OF GREAT TEACHERS, VOL-UME TWENTY-THREE (Book II)
By Elbert Hubbard
7⅝" x 5¾" 176 pages.
Body copy set in Old Style Antique.
Printed in two colors on Roycroft watermarked handmade paper with title page, initials, head and tail pieces designed by Dard Hunter.

166. LITTLE JOURNEYS TO THE HOMES OF GREAT TEACHERS
By Elbert Hubbard
Moses.
Printed in three colors on Roycroft handmade paper and bound in paper or boards. Designed by Dard Hunter.
Confucius.
(Same as above.)
Pythagoras.
(Same as above.)
Plato .
(Same as above.)
King Alfred..
(Same as above.)
Friedrich Froebel..
(Same as above.)
Booker T. Washington.
(Same as above.)
Thomas Arnold.
(Same as above.)
Erasmus.
(Same as above.)
Hypatia.
(Same as above.)
St. Benedict .
(Same as above.)
Mary Baker Eddy.
(Same as above.)

167. MAN OF SORROWS, THE
By Elbert Hubbard

7" x 4½" 121 pages.
Body copy set in Monotype Cushing.
Printed in one color with full color rendering of Christ by Gaspard tipped in.
Bound in paper boards with suede spine or stamped spine.

168. MESSAGE TO GARCIA, A Being a Preachment
by Elbert Hubbard
5½" x 4⅛" 19 pages.
Body copy set in Cheltenham.
Two color contents with one color title page. Bound in limp suede. Photo of
Elbert Hubbard opposite title page. Dated on title page December 1908.

169. ONE OF GOD'S NOBLEMEN (Abraham Lincoln)
By R. L. Sheldon
7¾" by 6" 34 pages.
Body copy set in Old Style Antique.
Printed in two colors on Boxmoor and paper bound. Press run unknown.

170. POEMS AND PLAYS OF WILLIAM SHAKESPEARE
7⅝" x 5¾" 56 pages.
Body copy set in Scotch Roman.
Printed on Boxmoor in brown ink. Bound in paper over boards with suede back
strap. No information on press run or binding variants. No information on com-
piler or source of compilation.

171. RECORD, A
Printed for F. L. Brown
7½" x 5¾" 26 pages.
Body copy set in Bookman. Bound in suede.

172. ROYCROFT SHOP-BEING A HISTORY, THE
By Elbert Hubbard
6" x 4½" 28 pages.
Paper bound.

173. RUBAIYAT OF OMAR KHAYYAM, THE
6" x 8" 71 pages. Body copy set in Bookman.
Dard Hunter title page, initial letters and colophon device. Printed in four colors on Roycroft watermarked laid paper and bound in either decorated suede or
paper over boards with suede backstrap.

174. RUBAIYAT OF OMAR KHAYYAM
5" x 8" 71 pages.
Body copy set in Cheltenham.
Four color Dard Hunter title page, initial letters and colophon device. It is
printed on Roycroft watermarked laid paper and bound in flexible decorated
leather, suede or paper over boards.This is similar at first glance to the previous
enby but the body type is different and the colophon statement of this edition is
set all caps whereas the colophon statement of the previous entry is set in caps
and lower case.

175. THREE GREAT WOMEN, Being Little Journeys
By Elbert Hubbard
8⅞" x 6⅞" 107 pages.
Body copy set in Cheltenham.
Printed on Boxmoor in three colors with initial letters designed by Dard Hunter.
Illustrations of Elbert Hubbard and essay subjects by Mazzanovich and
Gaspard. Bindings are paper over boards with suede spine or pigskin.

176. WOMAN'S WORK
By Alice Hubbard
8⅛" x 6¼" 157 pages.
Body copy set in Monotype 139.
Printed in two colors, green and ochre, on Boxmoor. Cover, title page, running
heads, tails and colophon designed by Dard Hunter. Bindings were paper
boards with cloth spine, suede, Alicia, modeled leather, 3/4 leather and one
known copy in full leather. There is an unlimited edition printed on Japan
Vellum offered in the same range of bindings noted above. Page size is 53/4" x
73/4". No change in collation or text design.

1909
177. BOOK OF DAYS, A
By F. Sydnor Cartmell
6⅞" x 4⅜" 59 pages.
Body copy set in Scotch Roman.
Two color printing of Roycroft watermarked paper. Bound in suede.

178. COMPLETE WRITINGS OF ELBERT HUBBARD, THE
(See 1908 for specifications)
Volume Five, 360 pages.
Volume Six, 362 pages.
Volume Seven, 381 pages.

179. DOCTORS, THE
A Satire in Four Seizures
By Elbert Hubbard
7¾" x 5¾" 123 pages.
Body copy set in Elzevir.
Printed in two colors on Boxmoor with two color illustrations by Burt Barnes on
butcher's paper inserted throughout the text. Title page and running calligraphic heads look like Dard Hunter's work but are unsigned. Bound in blind
stamped suede or sheep skin with woven hemp straps.

180. LIFE LESSONS
By Alice Hubbard
9" x 6¾" 194 pages.
Body copy set in Monotype 97J
Title page, initials and ornaments designed by Dard Hunter. Typography by
Charles Rosen. Photo engravings of sketches by Schnieder (erroneously noted as

Gaspard in 1909 catalog.) Printed in three colors on Boxmoor. An unnumbered edition was printed on Japan Vellum. Available bound in paper boards with suede spine, 3/4 leather, Alicia and full levant. This is the only work that has Dard Hunter's name in the colophon.

181. LITTLE JOURNEYS TO THE HOMES OF GREAT BUSINESSMEN, VOLUME TWENTY-FOUR (Book 1)
By Elbert Hubbard
7⅝" x 5¾" 220 pages.
Body copy set in Monotype Cushing.
Printed in four colors on Boxmoor. Title page, initials, borders, heads, tails designed by Dard Hunter.

182. LITTLE JOURNEYS TO THE HOMES OF GREAT BUSINESSMEN, VOLUME TWENTY-FIVE (Book ll)
By Elbert Hubbard
7⅝"x 5¾" 221 pages.
Body copy set in Monotype Cushing.
Printed in four colors on Boxmoor. Title page, initials, borders, heads, tails designed by Dard Hunter.

183. LITTLE JOURNEYS TO THE HOMES OF GREAT BUSINESSMEN
By Elbert Hubbard
Robert Owen.
Printed in four colors on Boxmoor and bound in paper or boards. Designed by Dard Hunter.
James Oliver.
(Same as above.)
Stephen Girard.
(Same as above.)
MayerA. Rothschild.
(Same as above.)
Philip D. Armour.
(Same as above.)
John Jacob Astor.
(Same as above.)
Peter Cooper.
(Same as above.)
Andrew Carnegie.
(Same as above.)
George Peabody.
(Same as above.)
A. T. Stewart.
(Same as above.)
H. H. Rogers..
(Same as above.)
James J. Hill
(Same as above.)

184. MOTTO BOOK, THE
Being a Catalogue of Epigrams
By Fra Elbertus (Elbert Hubbard) and Others
8" x 6" 58 pages.
Body copy set in Bookman.
Cover design by Dard Hunter in three colors. Interior printed in three colors
though not the same as cover. Cover design shows a new softer design
approach by Hunter, and only the lettering style is familiar. Interior shows
many of the motto designs for sale by the Roycrofters. Many of these are also
Dard Hunter designs.

185. TALE OF TWO TAILORS, A
By Elbert Hubbard
7" x 4½" 29 pages.
Body copy set in Cheltenham.
1500 copies printed in three colors on Boxmoor. Title page, initial letters and
decorations by Dard Hunter (from "White Hyacinths"). Bound in paper boards
with cloth spine. Cover calligraphy by Dard Hunter. This was an advertisement
and endorsement for a clothing manufacturer, Nathan Stein. The other tailor of
the title is Andrew Johnson who left the trade to pursue politics.

186. TALKS ON SOME FUNDAMENTALS OF EXPRESSION
By Leland Powers and Carol Hoyt Powers
6⅞" x 4½" 61 pages.
Body copy set in Caslon Bold.
Printed on Boxmoor and bound in paper boards with cloth spine.

187. TWO DEMANDS
By F. Sydnor Cartmell
8" x 5⅝" 151 pages.
Body copy set in Scotch Roman.
Printed in two colors. Two photo illustrations printed in two colors on coated
stock. Bindings are paper and paper boards.

1910
188. CLEVELAND MEN IN CARICATURE
10½" x 8" 396 pages
Body copy set in Old Style Antique Ink drawings of prominent men of that city
as done for Rochester and Louisville. Bound in suede.

189. FRIENDSHIP, LOVE AND MARRIAGE
By Henry David Thoreau
8¼" x 5¼" 55 pages.
Body copy set in Monotype 97J
Printed in one color on Roycroft watermarked Fabriano. Some copies have hand
colored title page, initial letters and colophon device after designs by Raymond
Nott. Bound in suede or paper over boards with cloth spine. There are the usual
variant bindings including some in vellum.

190. INTERVIEW, AN
By Sophie Irene Loeb
- and -
THE BASIS OF MARRIAGE
By Alice Hubbard
7¾" x 5¾" 21 pages
Body copy set in Cushing.
Printed in two colors with photogravure of Alice Hubbard. Paper bound with Dard Hunter cover design or in suede without Dard Hunter design.

191. LITTLE JOURNEYS TO THE HOMES OF GOOD MEN AND GREAT-MIRIAM EDITION
By Elbert Hubbard
7¾" x 5½" Volume one -143 pages
Volume two -167 pages.
Body copy set in Cushing.
Printed in one color on Roycroft watermarked paper. Bound in paper over boards with stamped leather spine. This Miriam binding became a standard Roycroft offering. A reprint of one of the original/ C. Putnam Little Journeys.

192. MANHATTAN/HENRY HUDSON
By Joseph 1. C. Clarke and Elbert Hubbard
7¾" x 5¹⁵⁄₁₆" 62 pages.
Body copy set in Cheltenham.
Printed in two colors, black and orange, on Roycroft watermarked paper. Cover and title page designed in three colors by Dard Hunter. Bound in paper over boards.

193. MINTAGE/BEING TEN STORIES AND ONE MORE, THE
By Elbert Hubbard
7⅛" x 4½" 132 pages.
Body copy set in Scotch Roman.
Title page, decorated initials and tailpieces designed by Dard Hunter. Printed in one color on Roycroft watermarked paper or on Japan Vellum. Photogravure of drawing of Elbert Hubbard in sepia on sepia calendared stock as frontispiece. Bound in paper boards with paper label. Also bound in Alicia and full suede.

1911
194. AMERICAN BIBLE, AN
Edited by Alice Hubbard
7¼" x 4⅞" 444 pages.
Body copy set in Bookman. Printed in two colors on unmarked laid paper. Bound in pigskin. Cover design has the look of Dard Hunter's work.

195. COMPLETE WRITINGS OF ELBERT HUBBARD, THE
Volume ten, 296 pages.
Volume eleven, 315 pages.

196. FOUR GOSPELS, THE
By Marilla Ricker
7" x 4½" 130 pages.
Body copy set in Scotch Roman.
Printed in two colors on Boxmoor and bound in paper over boards with leather spine. Frontispiece illustration of Ricker.

197. IDEAL WOMEN, THE
By Julia Frances Hubbard
7⅝" x 5¾" 13 pages.
Printed in two colors on Roycroft paper with mounted photo illustrations. Diverse bindings issued.

198. LINCOLN CENTENNIAL ASSOCIATION ADDRESS, THIRD ANNUAL MEETING
9¼" x 7" 56 pages.
Printed in one color on Roycroft handmade paper with photogravure on vellum tipped in. Bound in boards. A well done typographical piece.

199. LITTLE JOURNEYS TO THE HOMES OF GREAT BUSINESSMEN: JOHN B. STETSON
By Elbert Hubbard
7¾" x 5¾" 52 pages.
Body copy set in Monotype Cushing.
Printed in four colors on Boxmoor using the Dard Hunter designs. Originally used in the Little Journey to Great Business Men series of 1909. This is essentially an advertising endorsement, but since it was not commissioned by Stetson or his company we will treat it as a product of the Press.

200. LONG ROLL, THE
Being a Journal of the Civil War as set down by Charles F. Johnson - Sometimes of Hawkins Zouaves
7¾" x 5¾" 241 pages.
Body copy set in Scotch Roman.
Limiting statement notes that this is the "Duluth Edition - 500 copies are being printed by Elbert Hubbard. Another vanity printing by the press but an interesting Civil War history that is quite scarce and very much sought after by Civil War historians.

201. THOUSAND AND ONE EPIGRAMS, A
By Elbert Hubbard
6" x 4½" 186 pages.
Body copy set in Scotch Roman.
Printed in two colors on Roycroft watermarked laid paper and bound in modeled leather, paper over boards or 3/4 levant. No limitation statement.

202. AMERICAN BIBLE, AN
Edited by Alice Hubbard
9⅞" x 7⅛" 328 pages
Body copy set in Bookman.
Regular edition printed in two colors on Strathmore with photogravure sketches of essayists on vellum. Bound in flexible leather, gold stamped. Contents identical to 1911 edition but this tall edition differs completely in make up and decoration. Design work could be Dard Hunter's but is unsigned.

203. ANDREW TAYLOR STILL/Being a Little Journey to the Home of the Founder of Osteopathy
By Elbert Hubbard
7¾" x 5¾" 28 pages.
Body copy set in Bookman.
Printed in two colors on Boxmoor, photo illustrated and bound in suede. This is one of the commercial Little Journeys.

204. BOYCOTT OF AUTOLOGY, THE
By Anna Stamm Morris with an introductory essay by Elbert Hubbard   46 pages of two color printing; paper bound.

205. CLUBMEN OF LOUISVILLE IN CARICATURE AND VERSE
Drawings by P. A. Plaschke and Associated Artists. Verses by Charles Hamilton Musgrove.
10⅜" x 8" 243 pages excluding roster. Suede bound.

206. COMPLETE WRITINGS OF ELBERT HUBBARD, THE
Volume twelve, 316 pages.
Volume thirteen, 328 pages.
Volume fourteen, 295 pages.

207. FEATHER DUSTER, OR, IS HE SINCERE, THE
Being Three Criticisms and One More of East Aurora
by William Marian Reedy, Harold Bolce, Ben De Casseres and Brainard L. Bates
6" x 4" 102 pages.
Body copy set in Scotch Roman.
Printed on Old Stratford in two colors and bound in paper over boards or stamped leather. Photogravures of Elbert Hubbard and William Marian Reedy used as frontispiece.

208. HOLLYHOCKS AND GOLDENGLOW
By Elbert Hubbard
7¼" x 5" 158 pages.
Body copy set in Scotch Roman. Printed on Strathmore in one color and bound in paper over boards or stamped leather. Frontispiece portrait of Elbert Hubbard with printed border and signature. The title page is in the style of Dard Hunter but is unsigned. There is a limited edition of 1,000 signed in Elber Hubbard's name and bound in stamped leather.

209. MYTH IN MARRIAGE, THE
By Alice Hubbard
6" x 4" 79 pages.
Body copy set in Scotch Roman.
Printed in two colors on Old Stratford and bound in blind stamped leather.
Cover typography by Dard Hunter. Title page, initials and ornaments designed
by Raymond Nott.

210. RUBAIYAT OF OMAR KHAYYAM, THE
6" x 3⅜" 54 pages.
Body copy set in Scotch Roman. Printed in two colors on Spanish laid paper
and bound in stamped leather. Interesting calligraphic title page.

1913
211. COMPLETE WRITINGS OF ELBERT HUBBARD, THE
Volume fifteen, 273 pages.
Volume sixteen, 314 pages.
Volume seventeen, 322 pages.

212. EVOLUTION OF A TEMPLE OF LEARNING, THE
By W. S. Lewis
6" x 4½" 30 pages.
Body copy set in Monotype Caslon Old Roman.
Printed in two colors on Boxmoor; bound in suede. Photo halftone tipped- in.

213. GARNET AND THE BRINDLED COW
By Alice Hubbard
9⅜" x 6" 24 pages.
Body copy set in Kennerly.
1003 copies printed on laid paper, French folded. Each volume is hand illumined and illustrated with four photogravures. Binding is marbled paper over
boards with leather quarter spine and corners. 400 copies printed on Japan
Vellum and bound either full levant or as above. Both editions were numbered
and signed by Alice Hubbard. This is one of the handsomest books of the
Roycroft Press but the heaviness of the binders board has caused most copies to
split at the hinges. You may encounter variants of this edition that lack the photogravures and have an Art Nouveau motif blind embossed in the leather binding These are remainders that were made up several years after the original
issue.

214. JOHN D. ROCKEFELLER, A LITTLE JOURNEY TO THE HOME OF
By Elbert Hubbard
11½" x 8" 44 pages.
Body copy set in Cheltenham.
Printed in three colors on Roycroft handmade paper and bound in paper over
boards with cloth spine. Photogravure of Rockefeller as frontispiece. Used the
layout designed by Dard Hunter for the Complete Writings.

215. TWENTIETH CENTURY MUSINGS
By M. Clay Burbridge
7½" x 5" 534 pages. Body copy set in Bookman.
Printed in one color and bound in suede.

1914
216. CLUBMEN OF ROCHESTER IN CARICATURE
Drawings by Sack Sears and Associated Artists
8" x 10" 350 pages excluding roster.
Bound in limp suede.

217. COMPLETE WRITINGS OF ELBERT HUBBARD, THE
Volume Eighteen, 304 pages.
Volume Nineteen, 304 pages.

218. GREAT LAKES, THE
By Anna Schoelkopf
6¼" x 4 ³⁄₁₆" 107 pages.
Body copy set in Scotch Roman.
Printed in two colors on Berkshire Text paper. Photo of Mrs. Schoelkopf as frontispiece with interior illustrations by Schnieder. Bound in decorated suede over boards.

219. LEST WE FORGET
By Ella Wheeler Wilcox
32 page paper bound booklet printed in two colors for the Thomas Paine National Historical Association.

220. MOTTO BOOK, THE
Being a Collection of Epigrams
By Fra Elbertus (Elbert Hubbard) and Others
7¹⁵⁄₁₆" x 5" 64 pages.
Body copy set in Bookman.
Regular edition printed in two colors on unmarked paper. Paper bound cover printed in three colors, red, green and black. An Art Nouveau denivabon that is quite handsome and reminiscent of Dard Hunter. It could be a copy of an earlier Hunter design. The press run is unknown, and there is the possibility of binding variations.

221. PIG PEN PETE OR SOME CHUMS OF MINE
By Elbert Hubbard
7¼" x 5⅛" 221 pages.
Body copy set in Monotype 78J.
Printed in two colors, black and orange, on Strathmore. Title page, initial letters and decorations by Dard Hunter (reuse). Photo illustrations. Regular binding was stamped leather. Copies were available in fine bindings and with hand illumination.

222. POEMS
By Theodora Goujard DeWolf Colt
8" x 5¼" 231 pages.
Body copy set in Scotch Roman.
Printed in two colors on laid paper.
This is one of the more interesting vanity pieces done by the Press. It is well
designed and on an exquisite soft laid paper. The paper lacks watermarks and is
not otherwise identifiable. This is one example of Roycroft printing and binding
at its best. Various bindings will be seen such as three-quarter leather, modeled
leather, etc.

223. ROYCROFT DICTIONARY, THE
Concocted by Ali Baba and the Bunch on Rainy Days
6" x 4" 172 pages.
Body copy set in Scotch Roman.
Printed in two colors, red and black, on watermarked machine made paper.
Bound in boards with cloth or leather back strip. Press run unknown.
There is an edition printed on Japan Vellum noted as a "few copies". None have
been located. The edition on regular paper and the edition on Japan Vellum
were also available bound in flexible leather, 3/4 leather and full levant.

224. TO LOVERS AND OTHERS
By Harry C. Morse
82 page booklet; paper bound or bound in gilt stamped leather.

225. WAYSIDE THOUGHTS
By Daisy Hubbard Carlock
6¼" x 4⅜" 47 pages.
Body copy set in Monotype 78J.
Daisy was Elbert Hubbard's sister. She was widowed in 1893, remarried in 1899
and died that same year.
a. Wayside Thoughts
By Daisy Hubbard C. Pollitt
Another issue with the name change only. We have placed this undated issue
with the 1914 entries by circumstantial evidence.

1915
226. ART AND ARCHITECTURE OR THE WORLD'S LOVE OF STONE
By Elbert Hubbard
8" x 5¾" 32 pages.
Body copy set in Monotype 78J.
Printed in two colors. Photoengraving of Cathedral of Rheims on coated stock
as frontispiece. Body paper stock is Roycroft watermarked Fabriano. Bound in
suede.

227. CIRCE
By Isaac Flagg
8" x 5¾" 178 pages.

Body copy set in Scotch Roman.
Private printing with four color frontispiece and two color paper bound cover.

228. COMPLETE WRITINGS OF ELBERT HUBBARD, THE
Volume Twenty (last volume of set).
Same size and binding style as previous volumes but different in typographical treatment and paper stock. Title page now classical   reproduction with Roman letters. Body copy set in two columns in smaller Cheltenham than previous volumes. Colophon states that the volume was finished August 14, 1915.

229. IN MEMORIAM: ELBERT AND ALICE HUBBARD
Collected and arranged by John T. Hoyle
7¼" x 5⅛" 358 pages.
Body copy set in Monotype 78J.
Printed in two colors, red and black, on machine made paper with Roycroft watermark. Decorated initials and tailpieces. Photo illustrated. Printing supervised by Charles Rosen; binding by Charles Youngers. Bound in stamped leather.

230. LIBERATORS, THE
Being Adventures in the City of Fine Minds
11½" x 7¾" 312 pages.
Body copy set in Cheltenham.
Printed in two colors on Roycroft handmade paper. Edited and arranged by John T. Hoyle with typography by Charles Rosen and Axel Sahlin. Presswork by John Hall and bound by Charles Youngers. Binding was paper over boards with modeled leather back strip and corners.

231. LITTLE JOURNEY TO THE HOME OF JAC AUER, A
By Elbert Hubbard
7¾" x 5¾" 24 pages (unnumbered).
Body copy set in Bookman.
Printed in two colors on Roycroft handmade paper and bound in suede. Illustrated throughout with photogravures of Auer's studio. This is another commercial Little Journey.

232. REDDY RINGLETS
By Elbert Hubbard
6" x 4¼" 21 pages.
Body copy set in Monotype 21E.
Printed in two colors on Japan Vellum with reproduction of painting by J. H. Harris as frontispiece. Bound in suede.

233. SAMUEL POMEROY COLT
By Elbert Hubbard
7¾" x 5⅜" 160 pages.
Body copy set in Bookman.
Same fine paper stock as Poems of 1914. Photo illustrated and bound in suede.

234. NAME THEY HAVE FORGOT
By Helen Finch Kasson

235. REVIEW OF THE BIBLES
By David R. Coughlin

1916
236. EVERYBODY'S BUSINESS
By Charles L. MacGregor

237. GRAVE DIGGERS, THE
By Fred Emerson Brooks

238. HOUSES OF CLAY
By Clay Morrison

239. I DON'T KNOW, DO YOU?
By Marilla Ricker

240. MAN OF SORROWS, THE
By Elbert Hubbard

241. PHILOSOPHY OF ELBERT HUBBARD, THE
A Compilation of Writing
7⅜" x 4¾" 174 pages.
Body copy set in Monotype 38E.
Three color printing on Roycroft watermarked laid paper. Bound in paper over boards. A well designed book and the only Roycroft publication that states that their handmade paper was made by Fabriano of Italy. The edition was "limited" to 9, 983 copies and was signed and numbered by Elbert Hubbard IL

242. POEMS AND ADDRESSES
By Rufus McQueen Gibbs

243. ROMANCE OF BUSINESS, THE
By Elbert Hubbard

244. UNFINISHED STORY, BY THE GENERAL MANAGER, AN
By W. Linton Smith

245. WAY OF THE TRANSGRESSOR, THE
By Harry V. Dougherty.

246. WHO NAMED YOU? A SUNDAY PASTIME
By Mrs. E. K. Smith

1917
247. COMPENSATION
By Ralph Waldo Emerson

248. CUSTER'S LAST FIGHT AT LITTLE BIG HORN
By Elbert Hubbard

249. DESERTED VILLAGE, THE
By Oliver Goldsmith

250. GOD I SEE, THE
By John B. Cable

251. 1 AM NOT AFRAID - ARE YOU?
By Marilla R. Ricker

252. IN THE SPOTLIGHT
Personal Experiences of Elbert Hubbard on the American stage Edited by John T. Hoyle
8" x 5¼" 134 pages.
Body copy set in Bookman. Two color printing on Roycroft watermarked paper. Bound in paper over boards with cloth spine.

253. ONE DAY - A TALE OF THE PRAIRIES
By Elbert Hubbard

254. RAVEN AND THE BELLS, THE
By Edgar Allen Poe

255. ROMANCE OF BUSINESS, THE
By Elbert Hubbard

256. ROYCROFT ANTHOLOGY, A
Selected and Edited by John T. Hoyle
9" x 6" 194 pages plus index.
Body copy set in Century Expanded Italic.
Printed in two colors on Roycroft watermarked paper and bound in marbled paper over boards with decorated leather spine and corners.

257. RUBAIYAT OF OMAR KHAYYAM Pocket edition

258. TO LOVERS AND OTHERS
By Harry C. Moss

1918
259. AMERICAN BIBLE, AN
By Alice Hubbard

260. MESSAGE TO GARCIA WITH AN APOLOGIA FOR WRITING THE MESSAGE
By Elbert Hubbard

261. MOTHER GOOSE RHYMES
Pictured by Edward G. McCandlish
10" x 8" 46 pages.
Copy appears to be hand lettered.
Done in full color illustrations. The illustrative style is quite mature but we can find no information on McCandlish. Binding is full color illustration over boards with blue cloth or leather spine. A second edition was printed in 1928 or 1929. This edition is conspicuously different from the first. It has a green cloth spine and is printed in predominantly green tints where this edition used blue as its base color. The paper stock here is almost a newsstock grade. Points of difference include extra pages of verse. These pages are disbursed throughout the book as two page spreads. The illustration facing the title page of the first edition is missing in the second and finally, the second edition is 1/4" shorter than the first edition. This book is now quite scarce though the press run for both must have been substantial The book was heavily advertised at its original time of issue and used as a premium for several years.

262. WAR DAY LYRICS
By John R. Clements

263. WEPT OF WISH-TON-WISH
By Harris T. Dunbar

1919
264. BOOK OF THE 11TH, THE
Unit history of the 11th Provisional Regiment

265. IN THE SPOTLIGHT
By Elbert Hubbard

266. LIBERATORS, THE
By Elbert Hubbard with revisions by Elbert Hubbard ll

267. LUCKY BAG, THE
Yearbook of the U. S. Naval Academy

268. RECORD OF A PRIVATE, THE
By Cassius P. Byington

269. ROYCROFT ANTHOLOGY, A
Edited by John T. Hoyle

1920
270. ABDUL BA HAS FIRST DAYS IN AMERICA
By Julia Thompson

271. ABE LINCOLN AND NANCY HANKS
By Elbert Hubbard

272. CANTEENING UNDER TWO FLAGS
By Doris Kellogg

273. DOCTOR'S DUFFEL BAG, THE
By M. Louise Hurrell

274. HOWITZER, THE
Yearbook of the U. S. Military Academy

275. JARS OF LIFE, THE
By Alfred Fritchey

276. LUCKY BAG, THE
Yearbook of the U. S. Naval Academy

277. MOTTO BOOK, THE
By Elbert Hubbard

278. SIGNS OF SUCCESS
By Dr. Hamilton Cameron

The next three titles are boxed as a set with each title glassine wrapped.

279. CONCERNING SLANG AND OTHER DROLL STORIES
By Elbert Hubbard

280. QUEEN OF THE PORCH AND OTHER DROLL STORIES
By Elbert Hubbard

281. TWENTY O'CLOCK AND OTHER DROLL STORIES
By Elbert Hubbard

1921
282. HOW TO ANALIZE PEOPLE ON SIGHT
By Elsie Lincoln and Ralph Paine Benedict

283. HOW TO REALIZE ON YOUR OWN PERSONALITY
By Elsie Lincoln and Ralph Paine Benedict

284. HOW TO UNLOCK YOUR SUBCONSCIOUS MIND
By Elsie Lincoln and Ralph Paine Benedict

285. HOW TO UTILIZE YOUR MIND
By Elsie Lincoln and Ralph Paine Benedict

286. IMMUTABLE LAW, THE
By Laura Cooke Barker

287. IMPRESSIONS
By Elbert Hubbard ll
A good source for the history of the shop and Elbert Hubbard.

288. LOYALTY IN BUSINESS
By Elbert Hubbard

289. MENTAL ANALYSIS
By Elsie Lincoln and Ralph Paine Benedict

290. OLYMPIANS, THE
By Elbert Hubbard

291. THINGS THAT LIVE FOREVER
By J. Wellen

292. TIME AND CHANCE
By Elbert Hubbard

1922
293. CHRISTMAS CAROL, A
By Charles Dickens

294. DOCTORS, THE
By Elbert Hubbard

295. DREAMS AND THEIR MEANINGS
By Elbert Hubbard ll

296.   POE'S TALES: A Selection

297. WORLD WAR AT ITS CLIMAX
By E. H. O'Hara

1923
298. ANOTHER LITTLE JOURNEY A Posthumous Manuscript
By Elbert Hubbard
6⅛" x 5" 28 pages
Published by Davis & Geck, Inc. from a manuscript of a Little Journey that
Hubbard had written for them but apparently never published.

299. BOOK OF THE ROYCROFTERS, THE
By Elbert Hubbard and Elbert Hubbard ll

300. ELBERT HUBBARD'S SCRAP BOOK
Small edition (9" x 6")
a. Large edition (10⅜" x 8½") in paper and
b. Large edition in buckram

301. FORBIDDEN FRUIT AND OTHER BALLADES
By Thomas Lomax Hunter

302. ROMANCE OF NIAGARA AND OTHER POEMS, THE
By William H. Decker

303. ROYCROFT DICTIONARY AND BOOK OF EPIGRAMS
By Elbert Hubbard

304. SERMONETTES
By H. D. De Wese

305. SILVER ARROW, THE
By Elbert Hubbard

306. TALE OF WANDERINGS, A
By Isaac Flagg

307. TITANIC, THE
By Elbert Hubbard

1924
308. BOOK OF THE ROYCROFTERS, THE
64 pages; leather bound.

309. CHAUTAUQUA
By George William Gerwig

310. DREAMS
by Olive Schreiner.
Limited to 1983 copies; numbered and signed by Elbert Hubbard II. Bound in paper over boards with suede back strap.

311. INNER MAN, THE
By Arthur G. Staples

312. LIBERTY OF MAN, WOMAN AND CHILD, THE
By Robert G. Ingersoll

313. POEMS
by Gracxe Healy Woodruff

314. POOR RICHARD'S ALMANACK AND OTHER PAPERS
By Benjamin Franklin

315. PORTAGE TRAIL, THE
By Mabel Powers

1925
316. CIVIL WAR IN AMERICA, THE
By Francis Wayland Adams

1926
317. MESSAGE TO GARCIA
By Elbert Hubbard
Reproduction of the original manuscipt on single vellum pages. Limited to 495 copies signed by Elbert Hubbard II. Bound in paper over boards with leather backstrap and boxed in folio. There is another unique copy with an original manuscript of The Express Company with penciled corrections by Elbert Hubbard bound in. Done for Larkin family. Elbert Hubbard II was having material like this done as one-of-a-kind offerings to raise money and as gifts to who supported the press financially.

318. ALI BABA
By Elbert Hubbard

319. OUR TRIP AROUND THE WORLD
By Elsie Lincoln and Ralph Paine Benedict

320. SERMON ON THE MOUNT, THE

321. TO LOVERS AND OTHERS
By Harry C. Morse

322. WHITE HYACINTHS
By Elbert Hubbard

1927
323. GLIMPSES BEYOND
By E. E. Lewis

324. IMPRESSIONS
By Elbert Hubbard ll
An enlarged edition with additional photos and text

325. MAN OF SORROWS, THE
By Elbert Hubbard

326. NOTEBOOK OF ELBERT HUBBARD, THE
By Elbert Hubbard

327. THE ROMANCE OF BUSINESS
By Elbert Hubbard

328. SELF-RELIANCE
By Ralph Waldo Emerson

1928
329. BRAINOLOGY
By Elsie Lincoln and Ralph Paine Benedict

330. HEAVENS PROCLAIM, THE
By Belle Bart

331. VALUE OF ESCHARTRIES, THE
By P. Nichols

1929
332. ADVERTISING AND ADVERTISEMENTS
By Elbert Hubbard A quarto of 276 pages plus index printed in two colors and bound in paper over boards with cloth spine. It is a collection of ads written by Hubbard that appeared in various Roycroft publications.

333. BUMPS: THE GOLF BALL KID AND LITTLE CADDIE
By V. McMahan

334. CHRISTMAS CAROL, A
By Charles Dickens

335. ELBERT HUBBARD I KNEW, THE
By Mary Hubbard Heath
This has variant bindings and an errata slip tipped in.

336. SHAKESPEARE'S IDEALS OF WOMANHOOD
By George William Gerwig

337. TEMPLED HILLS
By George W. Gerwig

1930
**338. GARDEN OF THE HEART FROM THE WRITINGS OF BA HA "u"
ABDU'L BA HA**
By Frances Esty
339. MORGAN EPISODE IN AMERICAN FREE MASONRY, THE
By Stanley Upton Mock

340. PHILOSOPHY OF ELBERT HUBBARD, THE

341. VALUE OF ESCHAROTICS MEDICINE, THE
By Perry Nichols
(This title was reprinted in 1931, 1932 and 1934)

1931
342. ELBERT HUBBARD - PIONEER ADVERTISING MAN
By Burton Bigelow

343. SILVER ARROW, THE
By Elbert Hubbard

1932
344. SONGS OF THE VINEYARD
By C. S. DeSilva

1933
345. BUNDLE OF OLD LETTERS, A
By Esther C. Davenport

346. ELBERT HUBBARD SPEAKS

1934
347. CHRISTMAS MESSAGE, A
By E. J. Kulas

348. JESUS - A SISTER'S MEMORIES
By George W. Gerwig

349. MOTHER GOOSE RHYMES
This edition differs from the 1918 edition in interior make-up. Best quick identification is the green spine of this edition.

350. SAMUEL J. MOORE AND THE SALES BOOK INDUSTRY
This volume is most interesting.It is a quarto of 64 pages printed in one color on
Roycroft handmade paper. There is a frontispiece photoengraving of Mr. Morse;
the typeface is Cheltenham and the initial/ letters are hand colored. It is very

well designed and printed and shows that the shop could still do excellent work at this late date. It also makes one wonder why more of this high quality work was not done. This piece was done for the Sales Book Manufacturers Association.

351. SONGS OF THE SESPE
By Frank D. Felt.

1935
352. THROUGH THE DOOR AND OTHER POEMS
By Barinda Barnes Ahrendts

1936
353. AURORAN, THE
(Class book of East Aurora High School)

354. EXPLOSIVE THEORY OF THE UNIVERSE
By William Henry Chambers. Limited to 1000 copies. Bound in paper over boards with leather back strap.

355. GOSPELS OF COURAGE
By Salle Dowman Caldwell

356. LIFE ETERNAL - EXCERPTS FROM THE WRITINGS OF BAHA LLAH AND ABDUL BAHA
By Mary Rumsey Movius

357. STANNINGLY MYSTERY, THE
By Matthew H. Calvert

1937
358. HISTORIC HOMES OF HAWAII
By Edna Williamson Stall

359. SEVENTY-FIVE YEARS OF THE FOUNDING OF THE BUFFALO HIS-TORICAL SOCIETY

1938
360. NO NEW FRONTIERS
By John Dun

1939
No titles discovered.
(The shop was supposed to be closed)

1940
361. EAST IS EAST AND WEST IS WEST
By Carlos Emmons Cummings

362. FRANCIS PARNELL MURPHY
By Samuel R. Guard and Lloyd Graham

363. ST. LAWRENCE SEAWAY, THE
By B. D. Tollamy and T. M. Sedweek

1941
364. BY THEIR WORKS
By H. Phelps Clawson
Printed for the Buffalo Museum of Science.

COLLATERAL MATERIAL

The Roycroft enterprises generated an enormous amount of advertising materi-al. Add this material to the pamphlets written by Elbert Hubbard as preach-ments and advertising for his own clients and one compiles a list as long as the press list.

I have only included the press catalogs, but those interested in other Roycroft wares such as copper ware, leather or furniture should try to obtain copies of the appropriate catalogs as reference tools.

Catalogs

The Roycroft Press catalogs are generally good reference material but should not be used as a guide to edition number nor advent of publication. They do have endorsements, articles, photo illustrations of Roycroft products and per-sonalities.

Most of the catalogs issued after 1900 were offered several times within a year or two with variant cover designs.

This list is not complete. It does include all of the catalogs that show new infor-mation. After 1910 much of the book advertising was done in The Philistine and Fra. Catalogs were revived by Bert Hubbard after 1915 and continued to be issued into the thirties.

1898

365. LIST OF THE BOOKS MADE BY THE ROYCROFTERS AT THE ROY-CROFT SHOP WHICH IS IN EAST AURORA, ERIE COUNTY, NEW YORK, MDCCCXCVIII, A

5⅝" x 4¼" 16 pages.
Self cover pamphlet printed in two colors and bound with yellow thread.

366. LIST OF THE BOOKS MADE BY THE ROYCROFTERS AT THE ROY-CROFT SHOP WHICH IS IN EAST AURORA, ERIE COUNTY, NEW YORK, MDCCCXCVIII, A

8⅛" x 5¼" 16 pages.
A large paper version of the above. The small paper edition is the first catalog issued by the press. This edition, with its brown paper cover is a later printing.

1899

367. SOME BOOKS FOR SALE AT OUR SHOP

8" x 6" 24 pages.
One color, red, on brown stock for the cover. Interior printed in two colors on Boxmoor and some copies are hand illumined. Thread binding.

1900

368. See entry 52 in major bibliography section.

1901
369. SOME BOOKS FOR SALE AT OUR SHOP
8" x 6" 14 pages.
One color, black, cover on brown cover stock. Interior printed in two colors on
Roycroft watermarked laid paper. Thread bound.

1902
370. SOME BOOKS FOR SALE AT OUR SHOP
8" x 6" 42 pages.
Cover printed in two colors on brown cover stock. Interior is printed in brown
and black with leaves of cover stock interspersed throughout the text having
halftone photographs of Roycroft personalities and facilities. Thread bound.

1903
371. SOME BOOKS FOR SALE AT OUR SHOP
8" x 6" 27 pages.
Cover printed in two colors on brown cover stock. Text is printed in two colors
with illustrations interspersed throughout. Bound in thread.

1904 -1905
372. SOME BOOKS FOR SALE AT OUR SHOP
8" x 6" 34 pages.
Two color cover on brown cover stock. Contents printed in three colors on
Roycroft wove paper. Photo illustrations bound in and printed on coated stock.
Thread bound.

1906
**373. A CATALOG OF ROYCROFT BOOKS AND THINGS - YEAR 10 FROM
THE FOUNDING OF THE ROYCROFT SHOP**
7 ¼" x 6" 26 pages.
A very different cover showing a pressman at the lever of a Washington hand
press over Dard Hunter calligraphic lettering.

**374. CATALOG OF SOME BOOKS & THINGS MADE BY THE ROY-
CROFTERS IN IDLE HOURS**
6¼" x 4" 32 pages.
Cover printed in two colors on Roycroft watermarked laid cover stock. Interior
printed in two colors on Roycroft watermarked handmade. This catalog offers
more than books. Thread bound.

1907-1908
**375. A CATALOG OF BOOKS AND THINGS CRAFT MADE BY THE ROY-
CROFTERS IN AN IDLE HOUR**
6⅝" x 4½" 30 pages.
Dard Hunter cover design. Two color interior and three color cover. Thread bound.

1909

376. THE ROYCROFT CATALOG
8" x 6½" 34 pages.
Dard Hunter cover design in three printed colors with the fourth color hand applied. Three color interior with bound in photo illustrations on coated stock. Thread bound. There is an interesting blind stamping on the cover.

377. THE ROYCROFT LEATHER BOOK
(Size) 46 pages.
Pictures and prices of their different leather goods available. Paper bound.

1910

378. A ROYCROFT CATALOG OF BOOKS, LEATHER, COPPER AND MOTTOS FOR 1910
8½" x 5¾" 128 pages.
Dard Hunter cover and title page designs with six order blanks bound into the back of the book and an index in the front of the book.
Bound in paper over boards with cloth spine.

Pamphlets
The following list is, I am sure, incomplete. Elbert Hubbard's greatest gift was his ability to write advertising copy and he wrote much for many.
The majority of these pamphlets have no historical value except to the student of advertising and its history. The Dard Hunter designs would be interesting to the student of graphic design history. I present them only as a guide to those who would enjoy collecting them. The majority were issued in two sizes: 8" x 6" and/or 6" x 4". The other pieces range below 6" x 4". Some are preachments, many are advertisements and many are that Elbert Hubbard specialty - the advertisement disguised as a preachment. Most were printed many times in different formats.

I have included pertinent information where available. Not all were dated and press runs are unknown. I have not seen every entry but have used titles recorded in the scant Roycroft records or recorded elsewhere. This will give duplication since I know that recorded titles were often short titles.
Pamphlets titled A Little Journey . . . have been placed alphabetically by key word such as Grapefruitola, A Little Journey to the Home of
Material such as the Little Journey to John D. Rockefeller, and such are placed here though they have more bulk than some of the material I have classified as literature.

I have used the guide of promotional goal or reading matter in placing some borderline material.

About Chalchikwill
An Adventure in Olive Oil
Advertising Ambassador
Age of the Auto (1910) (For U.S. Motor Co.)
Age of Rubber

Age of Steel

All's Well

An American Bible

American House, The

The Amencan National Assurance Co

America's Chance

Anatomik Commonsense Shoes

Appreciation, An *(About Mrs. Freda Ehmann and her Ehmann Olive Oil Company.)*

Arkansas and Its Great Health Resort - Hot Springs

Artistic Detroit

Atlas Press Clipping Bureau,

Aurora Colonial Furniture

BabcockElectrics (Cover and title page by Dard Hunter -1910)

Banks and Bankers

Barnaby Ginghams

Bartlett Book, The

Bigotry Bacillus, The (Cover and title page designed by Dard Hunter (1910)

Billmore, A Little Journey to

Blessed Damozel, The (1917)

Book of the Roycrofters, The (1928)

Bopp, Little Journey to the Home of

Boycott of Autology

Boy from Missouri Valley, The (Lettering by Dard Hunter on Cover)

B.P.O.E., Standard Metallic Co.

Breitmeyers

Brother to the Trees, A

Brownhill European Tours

Buffalo, A Little Journey to

Buffalo, Rochester and Pittsburgh Railroad, Little Journey Over the

Business Necessity, A

Business Progress and the Law

Cady Dental Company

Cairns of Saskatoon

Canton, A Little Journey to

Carnegie LibraryBuildings

Cash Friends

Catalogs, Little Journeys

Catalogs, Roycroft (See separate listing)

Central Manufacturing Anniversary Number

Central Manufacturing District, Little Journey to

Characters and Cars For Chalmers Automobiles n.d.

Hypositions

Imminence of the Postal Savings Bank, The

Impossible Guarantees

Interlaken School

Interview, An

Index to the History and Original Articles of Silas Hubbard, M.D. of East Aurora, Which is in Erie County, New York (1908) 12 pages.

Iroquois Catalogue

Is Christianity Declining? A Debate (1909)

Is It Concrete?

Jac Auer, Little Journey to the Home of (See 1915)

Joseph Dixon - One of the World-Makers (1912) by Elbert Hubbard

Judge of the Supreme Court

Jungle Book, The A Criticism by Fra Elbertus (Elbert Hubbard) 1906 copyright

Just Water (And How to Soften It)

Kalamazoo

Keep Cool

Kennicott Company, The

Keystone Travel Tour

Key to No. 72

Key to Success, The

Kingdom of Dust, The

Korry Krome Koruscation, A

Lamb School

Laundrys and Labels 1915

L. B. King & Company, A Little Journey to

Lectures by Alice Hubbard

Let Thrift Be Your Ruling Habit 1915

Lesson in Economics, A

Lest We Forget Little Journeys n.d. (Catalog for seAes)

Looking for Good Things (mentholatum)

Lunchful Liar, The

Lydia Pinkham 1915 by Elbert Hubbard

Maurice Baths, Little Journey to the 1913 rary Co., The

McCrary Co, The

McGarry, Garry

Mentholatum

Message to Garcia (See separate listing)

The copies of the Message to Garcia noted below are on ly a few of the many editions printed as pamphlets by the Roycroft Shop. The bound copies are listed in the bibliography. These are all pamphlets that have some uniqueness worth noting here. Remember that the Message was offered to all comers with the purchasers advertising message added.

Message to Garcia, A (January, 1904 Large pamphlet bound in dark brown Little Journey cover stock.)

Un Mensaje a Garcia (April, 1916 Small pamphlet bound in yellow-orange cover stock.)

Message to Garcia, A (1916 Butcher paper cover stock with imprint of Ithaca Gun Co., Ithaca, N.Y. Small pamphlet)

Message to Garcia, A (1916 Ivory color cover stock with Dard Hunter design. This pamphlet is imprinted 'Blue Bird Appliance Company, St. Louis, Mo., U.S.A.' Small pamphlet)

Message to Garcia (1917 Butcher paper cover stock with imprint of Wm. H. Wise & Co. on title page. Small pamphlet)

Message to Garcia (May 1917 Butcher paper cover stock with Dard Hunter cover design. Small pamphlet)

Message to Housekeepers, A

Message to Uncle Sam

Miller Train Control

Missouri Dairy Company, The

Modern Corporation Farming

Modern Homes Company of Ohio

Modern Laundry Methods

Modern Railroad, A Little Journey Over A

Monteith House

Mooseheart, A Little Journey to by Elbert Hubbard

Most Important Invention of the Times (The Miller Train Control)

Motto Book, The (1914, 64 pages.This early edition has an interesting cover design. These motto books were actually sales catalogs for Elbert Hubbard's epigrams.

Motto Book, The (1920) Contents similar to earlier edition. Cover and interior typographic make-up different. 67 pages.

Music at Meals A Musical Melange, or, A Little Journey to See Frank Hilton and Company

Mutual Life Insurance Co.

My Expensive Scrapbook

Neal Institure, A Little Journey to

Needs for the University

Neighborhood House, Review and Prospectus

New Science, or, the Art of Getting Well and Keeping Well, The

New York Railroad Company

No Drunkard Plan

Northwestern Ohio and Southern Michigan
One of God's Noblemen
One Man's Opinion (1907)
On the Road
Opportunities in Southwestern Ohio and Southern Michigan
Opportunity, Little Journey to Republic Club House (1914)
Optimist, The
Oral Righteousness As An Aid To Health and Happiness (1912) 32 pages.
Orpheum Vaudeville As I Have Found It by Elbert Hubbard
Our Telephone Service
Owl's Drug Companies, A Little Journey to the
Painless Dentistry - How it is Accomplished
Parcel Post
Pasadena
Pasteboard Proclivities
Pastelles in Prose (Cover, title page, heads, etc. by Dard Hunter For John
Wanamaker Co.)
Patrick Healy, Little Journey to
Peace, Poise & Power
Pebeco, A Little Journey to the Home of by Elbert Hubbard (toothpaste)
Pecomet
Peco Nut, Little Journey to the Home of
Peele Book, The
Photogravures of Great Men
Pickwick Licks
Pioneers
Pittsburgh Loxcmelera (?)
Pittsburgh Taxicab
Pittsburgh Taximeters
Plays
Politeness Pays
Pop Valve Pome (?)
Portfolio from Roycroft
Porte and Markle, A Little Journey to Porte and Markle Pivotal Points
Poser
Power - The Story of Niagara Falls (1914)
Profit Chokers
Progress
Prosperity Smiles
Purity and Progress Dard Hunter title page
Raiding a Railroad

Railroad Men, The

Raymond Riodon on Roycroft School of Life

Readable Write-ups (1909) 32 pages.

Refrigeration, Cold Storage and Ice-Making by Elbert Hubbard

Respectability, Restitution and Roofs

Reuther Potato Digger

Right Adjustment

Road to Success

Romance of the Railroad (1910) For Erie Railroad.(Unsigned Dard Hunter)

Royal Dane Milk and Cream Cans

Roycroft School of Life for Boys, The by Elbert Hubbard (1912)
Dard Hunter design cover

Roycroft Shop, The (1908) A History by Elbert Hubbard 28 pages.

Rules of Court

Salesmanship (by Hugh Chalmers)

San Mateo County, A Little Journey to

Saskatoon, A Little Journey

Save-All and Win-All Savings Bank

Science of Saving, The

Secret of Benjamin Franklin, The

Servia, A Little Journey to

Shoemakers, A Little Journey to

Shoes and Character

Silos and Which One Is Best

Simmonds Saws

Sir Roger de Coverly Papers (1917)

Smile Habits

Snap Shots and Education

Soap of Hope

Some Oxaline (Possibly Dard Hunter cover and title page)

Southern Disinfection Co., The

Spirit Teaching

Sponges and Pumice

Spring Tour

Standard Metallic Co.

Standard Oil Company (the Dard Hunter octopus cover.)

Standard Securities

Stetson, John B. A Little Journey to the Home of (See 1911)

Still, Andrew Taylor, Being a Little Journey to the Home of theFather of
Osteopathy (See 1912)

Story of Bread, The

NOTES

1. HUNTER, D. *Before Life Began,* Rowfant Club, Cleveland 1941

2. HUNTER, D. My *Life With Paper,* Alfred Knopf, 1958 quoted with permission of Cornell C. Hunter and Dard Hunter Jr.

3. CHAMPNEY, F. *Art & Glory* Crown Publishers, NY 1968 .

4. HAMILTON, C. *As Bees in Honey Drown,* A. S. Barnes, New Brunswick,(NJ) 1973

5. DIRLAM, K. & SIMMONS, E. *Sinners, This is East Aurora* Vantage Press, NY 1964

6. See HEATH, Mary Hubbard *The Elbert Hubbard I Knew,* The Roycrofters, East Aurora, 1931. This source backs up the various Hubbard reminiscences found in the *Phil,* etc.

7. *Buffalo News,* Buffalo, NY, December 9, 1902

8. Letter in possession of Nancy Hubbard Brady estate

9. *The Philistine,* April 1896

10. Elbert Hubbard II papers, Elbert Hubbard Museum, East Aurora, NY

11. *The Philistine,* January 1899

12. Copy in the Ernest Simmons papers, Buffalo and Erie County Public Library, Buffalo, NY

13. Copy in the Elbert Hubbard II papers, Elbert Hubbard Museum, East Aurora, NY

14. Original in Rare Book Department, The Free Library of Philadelphia. Quoted with permission.

15. Collection, Charles Burchfield Center, State University College, Buffalo

16. STALLMAN, R. W. *Stephen Crane, A Critical Bibliography,* Iowa State University Press, Ames, Iowa 1972

17. Photo copy in possession of author. The original was sold by Elbert Hubbard II to the Seven Gables Bookshop in 1962.

18. Elbert Hubbard II papers, Elbert Hubbard Museum, East Aurora, NY

19. WHITTINGTON-EGAN, R. and SMERDON, G. *The Quest of the Golden Boy,* Unicorn Press, London 1960

20. Letter from Harry P. Taber to *Saturday Review of Literature* October 16, 1926. Harry P. Taber papers, Buffalo and Erie County Public Library, Buffalo, NY

21. Collection of Charles Hamilton

22. KEMP, H. *Tramping On Life,* Boni & Liveright, New York 1922

23. Taped interviews now in the Rare Book Collection, Buffalo and Erir County Public Library, Buffalo, NY

24. Taped interviews now in the Rare Book Collection, Buffalo and Erir County Public Library, Buffalo, NY

25. Taped interviews now in the Rare Book Collection, Buffalo and Erir County Public Library, Buffalo, New York

26. Interviewed in Buffalo, NY 1976-80

27. Ernest Simmons papers, Buffalo and Erie County Public Library, Buffalo

28. Correspondence now in the Rare Book Collection, Buffalo and Erir County Public Library, Buffalo, NY

29. Elbert Hubbard II papers, Elbert Hubbard Museum, East Aurora, NY

30. See HUNTER, D. *My Life With Paper* for his account of his years at Roycroft.

31. See WOLFE, R. & MC KENNA, P. *Louis Herman Kinder and Fine Bookbinding America*, Bird and Bull Press, Newtown, Pa., 1985

32. Letter on Avena Shop stationary from Kinder to fellow binder. Copy now in the Rare Book Collection, Buffalo and Erir County Public Library, Buffalo, NY

33. See *A Bindery Goes to College, Bookmaking and Book Production*, August 1948

34. Letter in the archives of the Elbert Hubbard Museum, East Aurora, NY

35. Interviews with the daughters of Cy Rosen, East Aurora, NY, June 1976

36. HAMILTON, C. *An Exhibition/The Art of Samuel Warner/1872-1947;* Soenen/Wilmoth Booksellers, Clearwater, Fla. 1983

37. HUBBARD II, Elbert *Impressions*, Roycrofters, East Aurora, NY, 1921

38. Harry P. Taber papers, Buffalo and Erie County Public Library, Buffalo

39. Harry P. Taber papers, Buffalo and Erie County Public Library, Buffalo

40. Now the Buffalo and Erie County Public Library

41. BALCH, D. *Elbert Hubbard/Genius of Roycroft* New York, 1940

42. Harry P. Taber papers, Buffalo and Erie County Public Library, Buffalo

43. See Hamilton, C. *As Bees in Honey Drown*

44. *The Roycroft Shops, Being A History*, East Aurora, 1909

45. CHANDLER, L. *The Roycroft Shop*, 1912

46. Annual Reports, Roycroft Shops Inc. 1907-10. From the archives, Elbert Hubbard Museum, East Aurora, NY

47. William Marion Reedy in *The Feather Duster*, East Aurora, NY

48. FAXON, F. W. *Ephemeral Bibelots: A Bibliography of Modem Chapbooks and Their Imitators*

49. SHAY, F. *Elbert Hubbard of East Aurora*

50. Correspondence in Elbert Hubbard Museum, East Aurora, NY

51. HUBBARD II, E. *Impressions*, East Aurora, NY 1921

52. Correspondence in archives, Elbert Hubbard Museum, East Aurora, NY

53. VAIL, R. W. *A Message ιυ Garcia; A Bibliographical Puzzle* New York Public Library, NY 1930

54. Correspondence in archives, Elbert Hubbard Museum, East Aurora, NY

55. Now in the Rare Book Room, Buffalo and Erie County Public Library, Buffalo, NY

56. Elbert Hubbard Museum, East Aurora, NY

57. Elbert Hubbard Museum, East Aurora, NY

58. Copy in author's collection

59. See Wolfe/McKenna (item 31)

60. Taped interviews with author 1972-76

61. Taped interview, 1976

62. Harry P. Taber paper, Rare Book Room Buffalo and Erie County Public Library, Buffalo, NY

63. EVERITT, C. *Adventures of a Treasure Hunter*, Little Brown, Boston, 1951 quoted with permission of publisher

64. LANE, A. *Elbert Hubbard and His Work*, Worcester, Ma. 1901

Selected Reference

BALCH, David *Elbert Hubbard: Genius of Roycroft* Frederick A. Stokes New York 1940

BIGELOW, Burton *Elbert Hubbard: Pioneer Advertising Man* 1931

BONNELL, Cedric *An American William Morris and the Romance of the Roycrofters* 1904

Brihsh and Colonial Printer and Stationer Vol. 72, No. 3, Jan, 1913

CARUTHERS, J. Wade *Elbert Hubbard: A Case of Re-Interpretation* Connecticut Review, Vol. 1, No. 1 October 1967

CHAMPNEY, F. *Art & Glory* Crown Publishers N.Y. 1968

DIRLAM, K. & SIMMONS, E. *Sinners, This is East Aurora* Vanguard Press N.Y. 1968

FAXON, F. W. *Ephemeral Bibelots: A Bibliography of Modern Chapbooks and Their Imitators* F. W. FAXON Company London 1952

FAXON, F. W. *Bulletin of Bibliography, Vol. 3*, F. W. FAXON Company London May 1903

FRENCH, George *The American Printer, April 1902*

HAMILTON, C. *As Bees in Honey Drown* A. S. Barnes New Jersey 1973

HEATH, Mary Hubbard *The Elbert Hubbard I Knew* Roycroft Press East Aurora 1929

HUNTER, Dard *Elbert Hubbard and "A Message to Garcia"* The New Colophon, Vol. 1, Part 1 June 1948

HUNTER, Dard *My Life With Paper* Alfred A. Knopf New York 1958

HUNTER, Dard *Before Life Began* Rowfant Club Cleveland 1941

JAMES, W. Bevan *Elbert Hubbard, Master Man* C. W. Daniel, Ltd. London 1917

McGILL, Anna B. *The Roycrofters* Catholic World Sept, 1901

MOTT, Frank Luther *A History of American Magazines 1885-1905* Harvard Cambridge, MA 1957

SHAY, Felix *Elbert Hubbard of East Aurora* Wm. H. Wise & Company New York 1926

STALLMAN, R. W. *Stephen Crane, A Cribcal Bibliography* Iowa State University Ames, Iowa 1972

VAIL, R. W. *A Message to Garcia; A Bibliographical Puzzle* New York Public Library New York 1930

WHITTINGTON-EGAN, R. & SMERDON, Geoffrey *The Quest the Golden Boy, The Life and Letters of Richard LeGallienne* Unicorn Press London 1960

INDEX